FURTHER ADVENTURES OF LAD

Further Adventures
of Lad

ALBERT PAYSON TERHUNE

LIVING BOOK
PRESS

This edition published 2023
by Living Book Press
Copyright © Living Book Press, 2023

ISBN: 978-1-922919-94-6 (hardcover)
          978-1-922919-93-9 (softcover)

First published in 1922. The original, unabridged, text has been used which may reflect the language and attitudes of the time in which it was written.

NATIONAL LIBRARY OF AUSTRALIA

A catalogue record for this book is available from the National Library of Australia

MY BOOK IS DEDICATED
TO THE MEMORY OF

𝕷𝖆𝖉

THOROUGHBRED IN BODY AND SOUL

CONTENTS

The Coming of Lad   1

The Fetish   19

No Trespassing!   37

Hero-Stuff   59

The Stowaway   75

The Tracker   94

The Juggernaut   115

In Strange Company   133

Old Dog; New Tricks   158

The Intruders   176

The Guard   192

FOREWORD

Sunnybank Lad won a million friends through my book, "*LAD: A DOG*"; and through the Lad-anecdotes in "Buff: A Collie." These books themselves were in no sense great. But Laddie was great in every sense; and his life-story could not be marred, past interest, by my clumsy way of telling it.

People have written in gratifying numbers asking for more stories about Lad. More than seventeen hundred visitors have come all the way to Sunnybank to see his grave. So I wrote the collection of tales which are now included in "Further Adventures of Lad." Most of them appeared, in condensed form, in the Ladies' Home Journal.

Very much, I hope you may like them.

ALBERT PAYSON TERHUNE

"Sunnybank"
Pompton Lakes,
New Jersey

CHAPTER I.

THE COMING OF LAD

In the mile-away village of Hampton, there had been a veritable epidemic of burglaries—ranging from the theft of a brand-new ash-can from the steps of the Methodist chapel to the ravaging of Mrs. Blauvelt's whole lineful of clothes, on a washday dusk.

Up the Valley and down it, from Tuxedo to Ridgewood, there had been a half-score robberies of a very different order—depredations wrought, manifestly, by professionals; thieves whose motor cars served the twentieth century purpose of such historic steeds as Dick Turpin's Black Bess and Jack Shepard's Ranter. These thefts were in the line of jewelry and the like; and were as daringly wrought as were the modest local operators' raids on ash-can and laundry.

It is the easiest thing in the world to stir humankind's ever-tense burglar-nerves into hysterical jangling. In house after house, for miles of the peaceful North Jersey region, old pistols were cleaned and loaded; window fastenings and doorlocks were inspected and new hiding-places found for portable family treasures.

Across the lake from the village, and down the Valley from a dozen country homes, seeped the tide of precautions. And it swirled at last around the Place,—a thirty-acre homestead, isolated and sweet, whose grounds ran from highway to lake; and whose wistaria-clad gray house drowsed among big oaks midway between road and water; a furlong or more distant from either.

The Place's family dog,—a pointer,—had died, rich in years and honor. And the new peril of burglary made it highly needful to choose a successor for him.

The Master talked of buying a whalebone-and-steel-and-snow bull terrier, or a more formidable if more greedy Great Dane. But the Mistress wanted a collie. So they compromised by getting the collie.

He reached the Place in a crampy and smelly crate; preceded by a long envelope containing an intricate and imposing pedigree. The burglary-preventing problem seemed solved.

But when the crate was opened and its occupant stepped gravely forth, on the Place's veranda, the problem was revived.

All the Master and the Mistress had known about the newcomer,— apart from his price and lofty lineage,—was that his breeder had named him "Lad."

From these meager facts they had somehow built up a picture of a huge and grimly ferocious animal that should be a terror to all intruders and that might in time be induced to make friends with the Place's vouched-for occupants. In view of this, they had had a stout kennel made and to it they had affixed with double staples a chain strong enough to restrain a bull.

(It may as well be said here that never in all the sixteen years of his beautiful life did Lad occupy that or any other kennel nor wear that or any other chain.)

Even the crate which brought the new dog to the Place failed somehow to destroy the illusion of size and fierceness. But, the moment the crate door was opened the delusion was wrecked by Lad himself.

Out on to the porch he walked. The ramshackle crate behind him had a ridiculous air of a chrysalis from which some bright thing had departed. For a shaft of sunlight was shimmering athwart the veranda floor. And into the middle of the warm bar of radiance Laddie stepped,—and stood.

His fluffy puppy-coat of wavy mahogany-and-white caught a million sunbeams, reflecting them back in tawny-orange glints and in a dazzle as of snow. His forepaws were absurdly small, even for a puppy's. Above them the ridging of the stocky leg-bones gave as clear promise of mighty size and strength as did the amazingly deep little chest and square shoulders.

Here one day would stand a giant among dogs, powerful as a timber-wolf, lithe as a cat, as dangerous to foes as an angry tiger; a dog without fear or treachery; a dog of uncanny brain and great lovingly loyal heart and, withal, a dancing sense of fun. A dog with a soul.

All this, any canine physiologist might have read from the compact frame, the proud head-carriage, the smolder in the deep-set sorrowful dark eyes. To the casual observer, he was but a beautiful and appealing and wonderfully cuddleable bunch of puppyhood.

Lad's dark eyes swept the porch, the soft swelling green of the lawn, the flash of fire-blue lake among the trees below. Then, he deigned to look at the group of humans at one side of him. Gravely, impersonally, he surveyed them; not at all cowed or strange in his new surroundings; courteously inquisitive as to the twist of luck that had set him down here and as to the people who, presumably, were to be his future companions.

Perhaps the stout little heart quivered just a bit, if memory went back to his home kennel and to the rowdy throng of brothers and sisters and most of all, to the soft furry mother against whose side he had nestled every night since he was born. But if so, Lad was too valiant to show homesickness by so much as a whimper. And, assuredly, this House of Peace was infinitely better than the miserable crate wherein he had spent twenty horrible and jouncing and smelly and noisy hours.

From one to another of the group strayed the level sorrowful gaze. After the swift inspection, Laddie's eyes rested again on the Mistress. For an instant, he stood, looking at her, in that mildly polite curiosity which held no hint of personal interest.

Then, all at once, his plumy tail began to wave. Into his sad eyes sprang a flicker of warm friendliness. Unbidden—oblivious of everyone else he trotted across to where the Mistress sat. He put one tiny white paw in her lap; and stood thus, looking up lovingly into her face, tail awag, eyes shining.

"There's no question whose dog he's going to be," laughed the Master. "He's elected you,—by acclamation."

The Mistress caught up into her arms the halfgrown youngster, petting his silken head, running her white fingers through his shining mahogany coat; making crooning little friendly noises to him.

Lad forgot he was a dignified and stately pocket-edition of a collie. Under this spell, he changed in a second to an excessively loving and nestling and adoring puppy.

"Just the same," interposed the Master, "we've been stung. I wanted a dog to guard the Place and to be a menace to burglars and all that sort of thing. And they've sent us a Teddy-Bear. I think I'll ship him back and get a grown one. What sort of use is—?"

"He is going to be all those things," eagerly prophesied the Mistress. "And a hundred more. See how he loves to have me pet him! And, look—he's learned, already, to shake hands; and—"

"Fine!" applauded the Master. "So when it comes our turn to be visited by this motor-Raffles, the puppy will shake hands with him, and register love of petting; and the burly marauder will be so touched by Lad's friendliness that he'll not only spare our house but lead an upright life ever after. I—"

"Don't send him back!" she pleaded. "He'll grow up, soon, and—"

"And if only the courteous burglars will wait till he's a couple of years old," suggested the Master, "he—"

Set gently on the floor by the Mistress, Laddie had crossed to where the Master stood. The man, glancing down, met the puppy's gaze. For an instant he scowled at the miniature watchdog, so ludicrously different from the ferocious brute he had expected. Then,—for some queer reason,—he stooped and ran his hand roughly over the tawny coat, letting it rest at last on the shapely head that did not flinch or wriggle at his touch.

"All right," he decreed. "Let him stay. He'll be an amusing pet for you, anyhow. And his eye has the true thoroughbred expression,—'the look of eagles.' He may amount to something after all. Let him stay. We'll take a chance on burglars."

So it was that Lad came to the Place. So it was that he demanded and received due welcome which was ever Lad's way. The Master had been right about the pup's proving "an amusing pet," for the Mistress. From that first hour, Lad was never willingly out of her sight. He had adopted her. The Master, too,—in only a little lesser wholeheartedness,—he adopted. Toward the rest of the world, from the first, he was friendly but more or less indifferent.

Almost at once, his owners noted an odd trait in the dog's nature. He would of course get into any or all of the thousand mischief-scrapes which are the heritage of puppies. But, a single reproof was enough to cure him forever of the particular form of mischief which had just been chidden. He was one of those rare dogs that learn the Law by instinct; and that remember for all time a command or a prohibition once given them.

For example:—On his second day at the Place, he made a furious rush at a neurotic mother hen and her golden convoy of chicks. The Mistress,—luckily for all concerned,—was within call. At her sharp summons the puppy wheeled, midway in his charge, and trotted back to her. Severely, yet trying not to laugh at his worried aspect, she scolded Lad for his misdeed.

An hour later, as Lad was scampering ahead of her, past the stables, they rounded a corner and came flush upon the same nerve-wrecked hen and her brood. Lad halted in his scamper, with a suddenness that made him skid. Then, walking as though on eggs, he made an idiotically wide circle about the feathered dam and her silly chicks. Never thereafter did he assail any of the Place's fowls.

It was the same, when he sprang up merrily at a line of laundry, flapping in alluring invitation from the drying ground lines. A single word of rebuke,—and thenceforth the family wash was safe from him.

And so on with the myriad perplexing "Don'ts" which spatter the career of a fun-loving collie pup. Versed in the patience-fraying ways of pups in general, the Mistress and the Master marveled and bragged and praised.

All day and every day, life was a delight to the little dog. He had friends everywhere, willing to romp with him. He had squirrels to chase, among the oaks. He had the lake to splash ecstatically in: He had all he wanted to eat; and he had all the petting his hungry little heart could crave.

He was even allowed, with certain restrictions, to come into the mysterious house itself. Nor, after one defiant bark at a leopard-skin rug, did he molest anything therein. In the house, too, he found a genuine cave:—a wonderful place to lie and watch the world at large, and to stay cool in and to pretend he was a wolf. The cave was the deep space beneath the piano in the music room. It seemed to have a peculiar charm to Lad. To the end of his days, by the way, this cave was his chosen resting place. Nor, in his lifetime, did any other dog set foot therein.

So much for "all day and every day." But the nights were different.

Lad hated the nights. In the first place, everybody went to bed and left him alone. In the second, his hard-hearted owners made him sleep on a fluffy rug in a corner of the veranda instead of in his delectable piano-cave. Moreover, there was no food at night. And there was nobody to play with or to go for walks with or to listen to. There was nothing but gloom and silence and dullness. When a puppy takes fifty cat-naps in the course of the day, he cannot always be expected to sleep the night through. It is too much to ask. And Lad's waking hours at night were times of desolation and of utter boredom. True, he might have consoled himself, as does many a lesser pup, with voicing his woes in a series of melancholy howls. That, in time, would have drawn plenty of human attention to the lonely youngster; even if the attention were not wholly flattering.

But Lad did not belong to the howling type. When he was unhappy, he waxed silent. And his sorrowful eyes took on a deeper woe. By the way, if there is anything more sorrowful than the eyes of a collie pup that has never known sorrow, I have yet to see it.

No, Lad could not howl. And he could not hunt for squirrels. For these enemies of his were not content with the unsportsmanliness of climbing out of his reach in the daytime, when he chased them; but they added to their sins by joining the rest of the world,—except

Lad,—in sleeping all night. Even the lake that was so friendly by day was a chilly and forbidding playfellow on the cool North Jersey nights.

There was nothing for a poor lonely pup to do but stretch out on his rug and stare in unhappy silence up the driveway, in the impossible hope that someone might happen along through the darkness to play with him.

At such an hour and in such lonesomeness, Lad would gladly have tossed aside all prejudices of caste,—and all his natural dislikes, and would have frolicked in mad joy with the veriest stranger. Anything was better than this drear solitude throughout the million hours before the first of the maids should be stirring or the first of the farmhands report for work. Yes, night was a disgusting time; and it had not one single redeeming trait for the puppy.

Lad was not even consoled by the knowledge that he was guarding the slumbrous house. He was not guarding it. He had not the very remotest idea what it meant to be a watchdog. In all his five months he had never learned that there is unfriendliness in the world; or that there is anything to guard a house against.

True, it was instinctive with him to bark when People came down the drive, or appeared at the gates without warning. But more than once the Master had bidden him be silent when a rackety Puppy salvo of barking had broken in on the arrival of some guest. And Lad was still in perplexed doubt as to whether barking was something forbidden or merely limited.

One night,—a solemn, black, breathless August night, when half-visible heat lightning turned the murk of the western horizon to pulses of dirty sulphur, Lad awoke from a fitful dream of chasing squirrels which had never learned to climb.

He sat up on his rug, blinking around through the gloom in the half hope that some of those non-climbing squirrels might still be in sight. As they were not, he sighed unhappily and prepared to lay his classic young head back again on the rug for another spell of night-shortening sleep.

But, before his head could touch the rug, he reared it and half of his small body from the floor and focused his nearsighted eyes on the driveway. At the same time, his tail began to wag a thumping welcome.

Now, by day, a dog cannot see so far nor so clearly as can a human. But by night,—for comparatively short distances,—he can see much better than can his master. By day or by darkness, his keen hearing and keener scent make up for all defects of eyesight.

And now three of Lad's senses told him he was no longer alone in his tedious vigil. Down the drive, moving with amusing slowness and silence, a man was coming. He was on foot. And he was fairly well dressed. Dogs, the foremost snobs in creation,—are quick to note the difference between a well-clad and a disreputable stranger.

Here unquestionably was a visitor:—some such man as so often came to the Place and paid such flattering attention to the puppy. No longer need Lad be bored by the solitude of this particular night. Someone was coming towards the house;—and carrying a small bag under his arm. Someone to make friends with. Lad was very happy.

Deep in his throat a welcoming bark was born. But he stilled it. Once, when he had barked at the approach of a stranger, the stranger had gone away. If this stranger were to go away, all the night's fun would go with him. Also, no later than yesterday, the Master had scolded Lad for barking at a man who had called. Wherefore the dog held his peace.

Getting to his feet and stretching himself, fore and aft, in true collie fashion, the pup gamboled up the drive to meet the visitor.

The man was feeling his way through the pitch darkness, groping cautiously; halting once or twice for a smolder of lightning to silhouette the house he was nearing. In a wooded lane, a quarter mile away, his lightless motor car waited.

Lad trotted up to him, the tiny white feet noiseless in the soft dust of the drive. The man did not see him, but passed so close to the dog's hospitably upthrust nose that he all but touched it.

Only slightly rebuffed at such chill lack of cordiality, Lad fell in behind him, tail awag, and followed him to the porch. When the guest should ring the bell, the Master or one of the maids would come to the door. There would be lights and talk; and perhaps Laddie himself might be allowed to slip in to his beloved cave.

But the man did not ring. He did not stop at the door at all. On tiptoe he skirted the veranda to the old-fashioned bay windows at the south side of the living room; windows with catches as old-fashioned and as simple to open as themselves.

Lad padded along, a pace or so to the rear;—still hopeful of being petted or perhaps even romped with. The man gave a faint but promising sign of intent to romp, by swinging his small and very shiny brown bag to and fro as he walked. Thus ever did the Master swing Lad's precious canton flannel doll before throwing it for him to retrieve. Lad made a tentative snap at the bag, his tail wagging harder than ever. But he missed it. And, in another moment the man stopped swinging the bag and tucked it under his arm again as he began to mumble with a bit of steel.

There was the very faintest of clicks. Then, noiselessly the window slid upward. A second fumbling sent the wooden inside shutters ajar. The man worked with no uncertainty. Ever since his visit to the Place, a week earlier, behind the aegis of a big and bright and newly forged telephone-inspector badge, he had carried in his trained memory the location of windows and of obstructing furniture and of the primitive small safe in the living room wall, with its pitifully pickable lock;—the safe wherein the Place's few bits of valuable jewelry and other compact treasures reposed at night.

Lad was tempted to follow the creeping body and the fascinatingly swinging bag indoors. But his one effort to enter the house,—with muddy paws,—by way of an open window, had been rebuked by the Lawgivers. He had been led to understand that really well-bred little dogs come in by way of the door; and then only on permission.

So he waited, doubtfully, at the veranda edge; in the hope that his new friend might reappear or that the Master might perhaps want to show off his pup to the caller, as so often the Master was wont to do.

Head cocked to one side, tulip ears alert, Laddie stood listening. To the keenest human ears the thief's soft progress across the wide living room to the wall-safe would have been all but inaudible. But Lad could follow every phase of it; the cautious skirting of each chair; the hesitant pause as a bit of ancient furniture creaked; the halt in front of the safe; the queer grinding noise, muffled but persevering, at the lock; then the faint creak of the swinging iron door, and the deft groping of fingers.

Soon, the man started back toward the pale oblong of gloom which marked the window's outlines from the surrounding black. Lad's tail began to wag again. Apparently, this eccentric person was coming out, after all, to keep him company. Now, the man was kneeling on the window-seat. Now, in gingerly fashion, he reached forward and set the small bag down on the veranda; before negotiating the climb across the broad seat,—a climb that might well call for the use of both his hands.

Lad was entranced. Here was a game he understood. Thus, more than once, had the Mistress tossed out to him his flannel doll, as he had stood in pathetic invitation on the porch, looking in at her as she read or talked. She had laughed at his wild tossings and other maltreatments of the limp doll. He had felt he was scoring a real hit. And this hit he decided to repeat.

Snatching up the swollen little satchel, almost before it left the intruder's hand, Lad shook it, joyously, reveling in the faint clink and jingle of the contents. He backed playfully away; the bag-handle swinging in his jaws. Crouching low, he wagged his tail in ardent invitation to the stranger to chase him and get back the satchel. Thus did the Master romp with Lad, when the flannel doll was the prize of their game. And Lad loved such races.

Yes, the stranger was accepting the invitation. The moment he had crawled out on the veranda he reached down for the bag. As it was not where he thought he had left it, he swung his groping hand forward in a half-circle, his fingers sweeping the floor.

Make that enticing motion, directly in front of a playful collie pup; specially if he has something he doesn't want you to take from him;—and watch the effect.

Instantly, Lad was athrill with the spirit of the game. In one scurrying backward jump, he was off the veranda and on the lawn, tail vibrating, eyes dancing; satchel held tantalizingly towards its would-be possessor.

The light sound of his body touching ground reached the man. Reasoning that the sweep of his own arm had somehow knocked the bag off the porch, he ventured off the edge of the veranda and flashed a swathed ray of his pocket light along the ground in search of it.

The flashlight's lens was cleverly muffled; in a way to give forth but a single subdued finger of illumination. That one brief glimmer was enough to show the thief a right impossible sight. The glow struck answering lights from the polished sides of the brown bag. The bag was hanging in air, some six inches above the grass and perhaps five feet away from him. Then he saw it swig frivolously to one side and vanish in the night.

The astonished man had seen more. Feeble was the flashlight's shrouded ray, too feeble to outline against the night the small dark body behind the shining brown bag. But that same ray caught and reflected back to the incredulous beholder two splashes of pale fire;—glints from a pair of deep-set collie-eyes.

As the bag disappeared, the eerie fire-points were gone. The thief all but dropped his flashlight. He gaped in nervous dread; and sought vainly to account for the witch-work he had witnessed. He had plenty of nerve. He had plenty of experience along his chosen line of endeavor. But, while a crook may control his nerve, he cannot make it phlegmatic or steady. Always, he must be conscious of holding it in check, as a clever driver checks and steadies and keeps in subjection a plunging horse. Let the vigilance slacken, and there is a runaway.

Now this particular marauder had long ago keyed his nerve to the chance of interruption from some gun-brandishing householder;

and to the possible pursuit of police; and to the need of fighting or
of fleeing. But all his preparations had not taken into account this
newest emergency. He had not steeled himself to watch unmoved
the gliding away of a treasure-satchel, apparently moving of its
own will; nor the shimmer of two greenish sparks in the air just
above it. And, for an instant, the man had to battle against a craven
desire to bolt.

Lad, meanwhile, was having a beautiful time. Sincerely, he
appreciated the playful grab his nocturnal friend had made in his
general direction. Lad had countered this, by frisking away for
another five or six feet, and then wheeling about to face once more
his playfellow and to await the next move in the blithe gambol. The
pup could see tolerably well, in the darkness quite well enough to
play the game his guest had devised. And of course, he had no way
of knowing that the man could not see equally well.

Shaking off his momentary terror, the thief once more pressed
the button of his flashlight; swinging the torch in a swift semicircle
and extinguishing it at once; lest the dim glow be seen by any
wakeful member of the family.

That one quick sweep revealed to his gaze the shiny brown bag
a half-dozen feet ahead of him, still swinging several inches above
ground. He flung himself forward at it; refusing to believe he also
saw that queer double glow of pale light just above. He dived for
the satchel with the speed and the accuracy of a football tackle.
And that was all the good it did him.

Perhaps there is something in nature more agile and dismayingly
elusive than a romping young collie. But that "something" is not
a mortal man. As the thief sprang, Lad sprang in unison with
him; darting to the left and a yard or so backward. He came to an
expectant standstill once more; his tail wildly vibrating, his entire
furry body tingling with the glad excitement of the game. This
sportive visitor of his was a veritable godsend. If only he could be
coaxed into coming to play with him every night—!

But presently he noted that the other seemed to have wearied of the game. After plunging through the air and landing on all fours with his grasping hands closing on nothingness, the man had remained thus, as if dazed, for a second or so. Then he had felt the ground all about him. Then, bewildered, he had scrambled to his feet. Now he was standing, moveless, his lips working.

Yes, he seemed to be tired of the lovely game;—and just when Laddie was beginning to enter into the full spirit of it. Once in a while, the Mistress or the Master stopped playing, during the romps with the flannel doll. And Laddie had long since hit on a trick for reviving their interest. He employed this ruse now.

As the man stood, puzzled and scared, something brushed very lightly,-even coquettishly,—against his knuckles. He started in nervous fright. An instant later, the same thing brushed his knuckles again, this time more insistently. The man, in a spurt of fear-driven rage, grabbed at the invisible object. His fingers slipped along the smooth sides of the bewitched bag that Lad was shoving invitingly at him.

Brief as was the contact, it was long enough for the thief's sensitive finger tips to recognize what they touched. And both hands were brought suddenly into play, in a mad snatch for the prize. The ten avid fingers missed the bag; and came together with clawing force. But, before they met, the finger tips of the left hand telegraphed to the man's brain that they had had momentary light experience with something hairy and warm,—something that had slipped, eel-like, past them into the night;—something that most assuredly was no satchel, but *alive!*

The man's throat contracted, in gagging fright. And, as before, fear scourged him to feverish rage.

Recklessly he pressed the flashlight's button; and swung the muffled bar of light in every direction. In his other hand he leveled the pistol he had drawn. This time the shaded ray revealed to him not only his bag, but,—vaguely,—the Thing that held it.

He could not make out what manner of creature it was which gripped the satchel's handle and whose eyes pulsed back greenish flares into the torch's dim glow. But it was an animal of some kind;—distorted and formless in the wavering finger of blunted light; but still an animal. Not a ghost.

And fear departed. The intruder feared nothing mortal. The mystery in part explained, he did not bother to puzzle out the remainder of it. Impossible as it seemed, his bag was carried by some living thing. All that remained for him was to capture the thing, and recover his bag. The weak light still turned on, he gave chase.

Lad's spirits arose with a bound. His ruse had succeeded. He had reawakened in this easily-discouraged chum a new interest in the game. And he gamboled across the lawn, fairly wriggling with delight. He did not wish to make his friend lose interest again. So instead of dashing off at full speed, he frisked daintily, just out of reach of the clawing hand.

And in this pleasant fashion the two playfellows covered a hundred yards of ground. More than once, the man came within an inch of his quarry. But always, by the most imperceptible spurt of speed, Laddie arranged to keep himself and his dear satchel from capture.

Then, in no time at all, the game ended; and with it ended Lad's baby faith in the friendliness and trustworthiness of all human nature.

Realizing that the sound of his own stumblingly running feet and the intermittent flashes of his torch might well awaken some light sleeper in the house, the thief resolved on a daring move. This creature in front of him,—dog or bear or goat, or whatever it was,—was uncatchable. But by sending a bullet through it, he could bring the animal to a sudden and permanent stop.

Then, snatching up his bag and running at top speed, he himself could easily win clear of the Place before anyone of the household should appear. And his car would be a mile away before the neighborhood could be aroused. Fury at the weird beast and the wrenching strain on his own nerves lent eagerness to his acceptance of the idea.

He reached back again for his pistol, whipped it out, and, coming to a standstill, aimed at the pup. Lad, waiting only to bound over an obstruction in his path, came to a corresponding pause, not ten feet ahead of his playmate.

It was an easy shot. Yet the bullet went several inches above the obligingly waiting dog's back. Nine men out of ten, shooting by moonlight or by flashlight, aim too high. The thief had heard this old marksman-maxim fifty times. But, like most hearers of maxims, he had forgotten it at the one time in his speckled career when it might have been of any use to him.

He had fired. He had missed. In another second, every sleeper in the house and in the gate-lodge would be out of bed. His night's work was a blank, unless—

With a bull rush he hurled himself forward at the interestedly waiting Lad. And, as he sprang, he fired again. Then several things happened.

Everyone, except movie actors and newly-appointed policemen, knows that a man on foot cannot shoot straight, unless he is standing stock still. Yet, as luck would have it, this second shot found a mark where the first and better aimed bullet had gone wild.

Lad had leaped the narrow and deep ditch left along the lawn-edge by workers who were putting in a new water-main for the Place. On the far side of this obstacle he had stopped, and had waited for his friend to follow. But the friend had not followed. Instead, he had been somehow responsible for a spurt of red flame and for a most thrilling racket. Lad was more impressed than ever by the man's wondrous possibilities as a midnight entertainer. He waited, gayly expectant, for more. He got it.

There was a second rackety explosion and a second puff of lightning from the man's out-flung hand. But, this time, something like a red-hot whip-lash smote Lad with horribly agonizing force athwart the right hip.

The man had done this,—the man whom Laddie had thought so friendly and playful!

He had not done it by accident. For his hand had been out-flung directly at the pup, just as once had been the arm of the kennelman, back at Lad's birthplace, in beating a disobedient mongrel. It was the only beating Lad had ever seen. And it had stuck, shudderingly, in his uncannily sensitive memory. Yet now, he himself had just had a like experience.

In an instant, the pup's trustful friendliness was gone. The man had come on the Place, at dead of night, and had struck him. That must be paid for! Never would the pup forget,—his agonizing lesson that night intruders are not to be trusted or even to be tolerated. Within a single second, he had graduated from a little friend of all the world, into a vigilant watchdog.

With a snarl, he dropped the bag and whizzed forward at his assailant. Needle-sharp milk-teeth bared, head low, ruff abristle, friendly soft eyes as ferocious as a wolf's, he charged.

There had been scarce a breathing-space between the second report of the pistol and the collie's counterattack. But there had been time enough for the onward-plunging thief to step into the narrow lip of the water-pipe ditch. The momentum of his own rush hurled the upper part of his body forward. But his left leg, caught between the ditch-sides, did not keep pace with the rest of him. There was a hideous snapping sound, a screech of mortal anguish; and the man crashed to earth, in a dead faint of pain and shock,— his broken left leg still thrust at an impossible angle in the ditch.

Lad checked himself midway in his own fierce charge. Teeth bare, throat agrowl, he hesitated. It had seemed to him right and natural to assail the man who had struck him so painfully. But now this same man was lying still and helpless under him. And the sporting instincts of a hundred generations of thoroughbreds cried out to him not to mangle the defenseless.

Wherefore, he stood, irresolute; alert for sign of movement on the part of his foe. But there was no such sign. And the light bullet-graze on his hip was hurting like the very mischief.

Moreover, every window in the house beyond was blossoming forth into lights. There were sounds,—reassuring human sounds. And doors were opening. His deities were coming forth.

All at once, Laddie stopped being a vengeful beast of prey; and remembered that he was a very small and very much hurt and very lonely and worried puppy. He craved the Mistress's dear touch on his wound, and a word of crooning comfort from her soft voice. This yearning was mingled with a doubt lest perhaps he had been transgressing the Place's Law, in some new way; and lest he might have let himself in for a scolding. The Law was still so queer and so illogical!

Lad started toward the house. Then, pausing, he picked up the bag which had been so exhilarating a plaything for him this past few minutes and which he had forgotten in his pain.

It was Lad's collie way to pick up offerings (ranging from slippers to very dead fish) and to carry them to the Mistress. Sometimes he was petted for this. Sometimes the offering was lifted gingerly between aloof fingers and tossed back into the lake. But, nobody could well refuse so jingly and pretty a gift as this satchel.

The Master, sketchily attired, came running down the lawn, flashlight in hand. Past him, unnoticed, as he sped toward the ditch, a collie pup limped;—a very unhappy and comfort-seeking puppy who carried in his mouth a blood-spattered brown bag.

"It doesn't make sense to me!" complained the Master, next day, as he told the story for the dozenth time, to a new group of callers. "I heard the shots and I went out to investigate. There he was lying, half in and half out of the ditch. The fellow was unconscious. He didn't get his senses back till after the police came. Then he told some babbling yarn about a creature that had stolen his bag of loot and that had lured him to the ditch. He was all unnerved and upset, and almost out of his head with pain. So the police had little enough trouble in 'sweating' him. He told everything he knew. And there's a wholesale round-up of the motor-robbery bunch going on this afternoon as a result of it. But what I can't understand—"

"It's as clear as day," insisted the Mistress, stroking a silken head that pressed lovingly against her knee. "As clear as day. I was standing in the doorway here when Laddie came pattering up to me and laid a little satchel at my feet. I opened it, and well, it had everything of value in it that had been in the safe over there. That and the thief's story make it perfectly plain. Laddie caught the man as he was climbing out of that window. He got the bag away from him; and the man chased him, firing as he went. And he stumbled into the ditch and—"

"Nonsense!" laughed the Master. "I'll grant all you say about Lad's being the most marvelous puppy on earth. And I'll even believe all the miracles of his cleverness. But when it comes to taking a bag of jewelry from a burglar and then enticing him to a ditch and then coming back here to you with the bag—"

"Then how do you account—?"

"I don't. None of it makes sense to me. As I just said. But, whatever happened, it's turned Laddie into a real watchdog. Did you notice how he went for the police when they started down the drive, last night? We've got a watchdog at last."

"We've got more than a watchdog," amended the Mistress. "An ordinary watchdog would just scare away thieves or bite them. Lad captured the thief and then brought the stolen jewelry back to us. No other dog could have done that."

Lad, enraptured by the note of praise in the Mistress's soft voice, looked adoringly up into the face that smiled so proudly down at him. Then, catching the sound of a step on the drive, he dashed out to bark in murderous fashion at a wholly harmless delivery boy whom he had seen every day for weeks.

A watchdog can't afford to relax vigilance, for a single instant,—especially at the responsible age of five months.

CHAPTER II.

THE FETISH

From the night of the robbery, Lad's high position at the Place was assured.

Even in the months of ganglingly leggy awkwardness which generally separate furry puppyhood from dignified collie maturity, he gave sure promise of his quality. He was such a dog as is found perhaps once in a generation; the super-collie that neither knows nor needs such things as whip and chain; and that learns the Law with bewildering swiftness. A dog with a brain and a mighty heart, as well as an endless fund of loveableness and of gay courage.

Month by month, the youngster developed into a massive giant; his orange-mahogany coat a miracle of thickness and length, his deep chest promising power as well as wolflike grace. His mind and his oddly human traits developed as fast as did his body.

After the first month or so he received privileges never to be accorded to any other of the Place's dogs in Lad's lifetime. He slept at night under the music-room piano, in the "cave" that was his delight. At mealtimes he was even admitted into the sacred dining-room, where he lay on the floor at the Master's left hand. He had the run of the house, as fully as any human.

It was when Lad was eighteen months old that the mad-dog scare swept Hampton village; and reached its crawly tentacles out across the lake to the mile-distant Place.

Down the village street, one day, trotted an enormous black mongrel; full in the center of the roadway. The mongrel's heavy head was low, and lolled from side to side with each lurching stride of the big body. The eyes were bloodshot. From the mouth and the hanging dewlaps, flecks of foam dropped now and then to the ground.

The big mongrel was sick of mind and of body. He craved only to get out of that abode of men and to find solitude in the forests and hills beyond the village.

For this is the considerate way of dogs; and of cats as well. When dire sickness smites them, they do not hang about, craving sympathy and calling for endless attention. All they want is to get out of the way,—well out of the way, into the woods and swamps and mountains; where they may wrestle with their life-or-death problem in their own primitive manner; and where, if need be, they may die alone and peacefully, without troubling anyone else.

Especially is this true with dogs. If their malady is likely to affect the brain and to turn them savage, they make every possible attempt to escape from home and to be as far away from their masters as may be, before the crisis shall goad them into attacking those they love.

And, when some such suffering beast is seen, on his way to solitude, we humans prove our humanity by raising the idiotic bellow of "Mad dog!" and by chasing and torturing the victim. All this, despite proof that not one sick dog in a thousand, thus assailed, has any disease which is even remotely akin to rabies.

Next to vivisection, no crime against helpless animals is so needlessly and foolishly cruel as the average mad-dog chase.

Which is a digression; but which may or may not enable you to keep your head, next time a mad-dog scare sweeps your own neighborhood.

Down the middle of the dusty street trotted the sick mongrel. Five minutes earlier, he had escaped from the damp cellar in which his owner had imprisoned him when first he fell ill. And now, his one purpose was to leave the village behind him and to gain the leafy refuge of the foothills beyond.

Out from a door-yard, flashed a bumptious little fox terrier. Into the roadway he bounded; intent on challenging the bigger animal.

He barked ferociously; then danced in front of the invalid; yapping and snapping up at the hanging head. The big mongrel, in agony, snarled and made a lunge at his irritatingly dancing tormentor. His teeth dug grazingly into the terrier's withers; and, with an impatient toss, he flung the little beast to one side. Then he continued his interrupted flight; sick wrath beginning to encompass his reeling brain, at the annoyance he had encountered.

The yell of the slightly hurt terrier brought people to their doors. The sound disturbed a half-breed spaniel from his doze in the dust, and sent him out to continue the harrying his injured terrier chum had begun.

The spaniel flew at the black dog; nipping at the plodding forepaws. The mongrel raged; as might some painfully sick human who is pestered when he asks only to be let alone. His dull apathy gave place to sullen anger. He bit growlingly at the spaniel, throwing himself to one side in pursuit of the elusive foe. And he snapped with equal rage at an Irish terrier that had come out to add to the turmoil.

By this time, a score of people were dancing up and down inside their door-yard fences, squalling "Mad dog!" and flinging at the black brute any missile they could lay hand to.

A broken flower-pot cut the invalid's nose. A stone rebounded from his ribs. The raucous human yells completed the work the first dog had started. From a mere sufferer, the black mongrel had changed into a peril.

The Mistress had motored over to the Hampton post-office, that afternoon, to mail some letters. Lad, as usual, had gone with her. She had left him in the car, while she went into the post-office.

Lad lay there, in snug contentment, on the car's front seat; awaiting the return of his deity and keeping a watchful eye on anyone who chanced to loiter near the machine. Presently, he sat up. Leaning out, from one side of the seat, he stared down the hot roadway, in a direction whence a babel of highly exciting sounds began to issue.

Apparently, beyond that kick-up of dust, a furlong below, all sorts of interesting things were happening. Lad's soft eyes took on a glint of eager curiosity; and he sniffed the still air for further clues as to the nature of the fun. A number of humans,—to judge by the racket,—were shouting and screaming; and the well-understood word, "dog," formed a large part of their clamor. Also, there were real dogs mixed up in the fracas; and more than one of them had blood on him. So much the collie's uncanny senses of smell and of hearing told him.

Lad whimpered, far down in his throat. He had been left here to guard this car. It was his duty to stay where he was, until the Mistress should return. Yet, right behind him, there, a series of mighty entertaining things were happening,—things that he longed to investigate and to mix into. It was hard to do one's solemn duty as watchdog, when so much of wild interest was astir! Not once did it occur to Laddie to desert his post. But he could not forbear that low whimper and a glance of appeal toward the post-office.

And now, out of the smear of flying dust, loomed a lurching black shape;—gigantic, terrible. It was coming straight toward the car; still almost in mid-road. Behind, less distinct, appeared running men. And a shot was fired. Somebody had run indoors for a pistol, before joining the chase. The same somebody, in the van of the pursuers, had opened fire; and was in danger of doing far more damage to life than could a dozen allegedly mad dogs.

Just then, out from the post-office, came the Mistress. Crossing the narrow sidewalk, she neared the car. Lad stood up, wagging his plumed tail in welcome; his tiny white forepaws dancing a jig of eagerness on the leather seat-cushion.

On reeled the black mongrel; crazed by noise and pain. His bleared eyes caught a flash of the Mistress's white dress, on the walk, fifteen feet in front of him and a yard or more to one side.

In a frame of mind when every newcomer was a probable tormenter, the mongrel resolved to meet this white-clad foe, head-on. He swerved, with a stagger, from his bee-line of travel; growled hideously, and sprang full at her.

The Mistress paused, for an instant, in the middle of the sidewalk, to find out the reason for the sudden din that had assailed her ears as she emerged from the post-office. In that brief moment, she caught the multiple-bellowed phrase of "Mad dog!" and saw the black brute charging down upon her.

There was no time to dart back into the shelter of the building or to gain the lesser safety of the car. For the charging mongrel was not five feet away.

The Mistress stood stock-still; holding her hands at a level with her throat. She did not cry out; nor faint. That was not the Mistress's way. Like Lad, she was thoroughbred in soul as well as in body. And neither she nor her dog belonged to the breed of screamers. Through her mind, in that briefest fraction of a second whizzed the consoling thought:

"He's not mad, whatever else he is. A mad dog never swerves from his path."

But if the Mistress remained moveless, Lad did not. Seeing her peril even more swiftly than did she, he made one lightning dive from his perch on the car seat.

He did not leap at random. Lad's brain always worked more quickly than did his lithe body; flyingly rapid as were that body's motions. As he gathered himself for the spring, his campaign was mapped out.

Down upon the charging beast swooped a furry whirlwind of burnished mahogany-and-snow. Down it swooped with the whirring speed and unerring aim of an eagle. Sixty-odd pounds of sinewy weight smote the lunging mongrel, obliquely, on the left shoulder; knocking the great brute's legs from under him and throwing him completely off his balance. Into the dust crashed the two dogs; Lad on top. Before they struck ground, the collie's teeth had found their goal ire the side of the larger dog's throat; and every whalebone muscle in Lad's body was braced to hold his enemy down.

It was a clever hold. For the fall had thrown the mongrel on his side. And so long as Lad should be able to keep the great foaming head in that sideways posture, the other dog could not get his feet under him again. With his legs in their present position, he had no power to get up; but lay thrashing and snapping and snarling; and trying with all his cramped might to free himself from the muscular grip that held him prostrate.

It was all over in something like two seconds. Up stormed the crowd; the pistol-wielder at its head. Three shots were fired at point-blank range. By some miracle none of them harmed Lad; although one bullet scratched his foreleg on its way to the black giant's brain.

As soon as she could, the Mistress got herself and the loudly-praised Lad into the car and set off for home. Now that the peril was over, she felt dizzy and ill. She had seen what it is not well to see. And the memory of it haunted her for many a night thereafter.

As for Lad, he was still atingle with excitement. The noisy praise of those babbling humans had bothered him; and he had been glad to escape it. Lad hated to be mauled or talked to by strangers. But the Mistress's tremulous squeeze and her shuddering whisper of "Oh, Laddie! *Laddie!*" had shown she was proud of him. And this flattered and delighted Lad, past all measure.

He had acted on impulse. But, from the Mistress's manner, he saw he had made a wonderful hit with her by what he had done. And his tail thumped ecstatically against the seat as he cuddled very close to her side.

At home, there was more praise and petting;—this time from both the Mistress and the Master. And the Master bathed and patched the insignificant bullet-scratch on the collie's foreleg. Altogether, it was a gala afternoon for the young dog. And he loved it.

But, next morning, there was quite another phase of life awaiting him. Like most Great Moments, this exploit of Lad's was not on the free list. And Trouble set in;—grim and sinister trouble.

Breakfast was over. The Mistress and the Master were taking their wonted morning stroll through the grounds. Lad cantered along, ahead of them. The light bullet-scratch on his foreleg did not lame or annoy him. He inspected everything of canine interest; sniffing expert inquiry at holes which might prove to be rabbit warrens; glaring in truculent threat up some tree which might or might not harbor an impudent squirrel; affecting to see objects of mysterious import in bush clumps; crouching in dramatic threat at a fat stag-beetle which scuttled across his path.

There are an immense number of worth-while details for a very young collie, in even the most casual morning walk; especially if his Mistress and his Master chance to be under his escort. And Laddie neglected none of these things. If a troop of bears or a band of Indians or a man-eating elephant were lurking anywhere in the shrubbery or behind tree-trunks, Lad was not going to fail in discovering and routing out such possible dangers to the peace of mind of his two adored deities.

Scent and sight presently were attracted by a feeble fluttering under a low-limbed catalpa tree in whose branches a pair of hysterical robins were screeching. Lad paused, his tulip ears at attention, his plumed tail swaying. Then he pushed his long muzzle through a clump of grass and emerged carrying a flapping and piping morsel between his mighty jaws. The birds, on the limb above, redoubled their frenzied chirping; and made little futile dashes at the collie's head.

Unheeding, Lad walked back to the Mistress and laid gently at her feet the baby robin he had found. His keen teeth had not so much as ruffled its pinfeather plumage. Having done his share toward settling the bird's dilemma, Laddie stood back and watched in grave interest while the Mistress lifted the fluttering infant and put it back in the nest whence it had fallen.

"That makes the fifth baby bird Laddie has brought to me in a month," she commented, as she and the Master turned back toward the house. "To say nothing of two field mice and a broken-winged bat. He seems to think I'll know what to do for them."

"I only hope he won't happen upon a newborn rattlesnake or copperhead and bring it to you for refuge," answered the Master. "I never saw another dog, except a trained pointer or setter, that could handle birds so tenderly. He—"

The bumping of a badly handled rowboat, against the dock, at the foot of the lawn, a hundred yards below, checked his rambling words. Lad, at sudden attention, by his master's side, watched the boat's occupant clamber clumsily out of his scow; then stamp along the dock and up the lawn toward the house. The arrival was a long and lean and lank and lantern-jawed man with a set of the most fiery red whiskers ever seen outside a musical comedy. The Master had seen him several times, in the village; and recognized him as Homer Wefers, the newly-appointed Township Head Constable. The Mistress recognized him, too, as the vehement official whose volley of pistol-bullets had ended the sufferings of the black mongrel. She shivered, in reminiscence, as she looked at him. The memory he evoked was not pleasant.

"Morning!" Wefers observed, curtly, as the Master, with Lad beside him, stepped forward to greet the scarlet-bearded guest. "I tried to get over here, last night. But I guess it's soon enough, today. Has he showed any signs, yet?" He nodded inquiringly at the impassive Lad, as he spoke.

"'Soon enough' for what?" queried the puzzled Master.

"And what sort of 'signs' are you talking about?"

"Soon enough to shoot that big brown collie of yours," explained Wefers, with businesslike briskness. "And I'm asking if he's showed any signs of hydrophoby. Has he?"

"Are you speaking of Laddie?" asked the Mistress, in dismay; as the slower-witted Master, stared and gulped. "Why should he show any signs of hydrophobia? He—"

"If he hasn't, he will," rapped out the visitor. "Or he would, if he wasn't put out of the way. That's what I'm here for. But I kind of hoped maybe you folks might have done it, yourselves. Can't be too careful, you know. 'Specially—"

"What in blue blazes are you blithering about?" roared the Master, finding his voice and marshaling his startled wits. "Do you mean—"

"I mean," said Wefers, rebuking with a cold glare the Master's disrespectful manner, "I mean I'm here to shoot that big collie of yours. He was bit by a mad dog, yesterday. So was three other dogs over in the village. I shot 'em all; before they had time to d'velop symptoms and things; or bite anybody. One of 'em," he added, unctuously, "one of 'em b'longed to that little crippled Posthanger girl. She cried and begged, something pitiful, when I come for him. But dooty is dooty. So I—"

"*Oh!*"

The Mistress's horrified monosyllable broke in on the smug recital. She caught Lad protectingly by the ruff and stared in mute dread at the lanky and red-whiskered officer. Lad, reading her voice as always, divined this nasal-toned caller had said or done something to make her unhappy. His ruff bristled. One corner of his lip lifted in something which looked like a smile, but which was not. And, very far down in his throat a growl was born.

But the Master stepped in front of his wife and his dog, and confronted the constable. Fighting for calmness, he asked:

"Do I understand that you shot those harmless little pups just because a dog that was sick, and not rabid, happened to nip them? And that you've come across here with an idea of doing the same thing to Lad? Is that it?"

"That's the idea," assented Wefers. "I said so, right off, as soon as I got here. Only, you're wrong about the dog being 'sick.' He was mad. Had rabies. I'd ought to know. I—"

"How and why ought you to know?" demanded the Master, still battling for perfect calm, and succeeding none too well. "How ought you to know? Are you a veterinary? Have you ever made a study of dogs and of their maladies? Have you ever read up, carefully, on the subject of rabies? Have you read Eberhardt or Dr. Bennett or Skinner or any of a dozen other authorities on the disease? Have you consulted such eminent vets as Hopper and Finch, for instance? If you have, you certainly must know that a dog, afflicted with genuine rabies, will no more turn out of his way to bite anyone than a typhoid patient will jump out of bed to chase a doctor. I'm not saying that the bite of any sick animal (or of any sick human, for that matter) isn't more or less dangerous; unless it's carefully washed out and painted with iodine. But that's no excuse to go around the country, shooting every dog that some sick mongrel has snapped at. Put such dogs under observation, if necessary; and then—"

"You talk like a fool!" snorted Wefers, in lofty contempt. "I—"

"But I am going to keep you from acting like a fool," returned the Master, his hard-held temper beginning to fray. "You say you've come over here to shoot my dog. If ever anyone shoots Lad, I'll be the man to do it. And I'll have to have lots better reason for it than—"

"Go ahead, then!" vouchsafed the constable, fishing out a rusty service pistol from his coat-tail pocket. "Go ahead and do it yourself, then; if you'd rather. It's all one to me, so long's it's done."

With sardonic politeness, he proffered the bulky weapon. The Master caught it from his hand and flung it a hundred feet away, into the center of a clump of lilacs.

"So much for the gun!" he blazed, advancing an the astounded Wefers. "Now, unless you want to follow it—"

"Dear!" expostulated the Mistress, her sweet voice atremble.

"I'm an of'cer of the law!" blustered the offended constable; in the same breath adding:

"And resisting an of'cer in the p'soot of his dooty is a misde—"

He checked himself, unconsciously turning to observe the odd actions of Lad.

As the Master had hurled the pistol far from him, the collie had sped in breakneck pursuit of it. Thus, always, did he delight to retrieve any object the Mistress or the Master might toss for his amusement. It was one of Laddie's favorite games, this fetching back of anything thrown. The farther it might be flung and the more difficult its landing place, the more zest to the sport.

This time, Lad was especially glad at the diversion. From the voices of these deities of his, Lad had gathered that the Master was furiously angry and that the Mistress was correspondingly unhappy. Also, that the lanky and red-bearded visitor was directly responsible for their stress of feeling. He had been eyeing alternately the Master and Wefers; tensely awaiting some overt act or some word of permission which should warrant him in launching himself on the intruder.

And now, it seemed, the whole thing was a game;—a game wherein he himself had been invited to play a merry and spectacular part. Joyously, he flew after the hurtling lump of steel and rubber.

The Master, facing the constable, did not see his pet's performance. He took up the thread of speech where Wefers dropped it.

"I don't know what the law does or doesn't empower you to do, in such cases," he said, trying to force his way back to the earlier semblance of calm. "But I doubt if it permits you to trespass on my land, without a warrant or a court order of some sort; or to shoot a dog of mine. And, until I find out the law in the matter, you'll get off this place and keep off of it. As for the dog, I'll be legally responsible for him; and I'll guarantee he'll do no damage. So—"

Like Wefers, the Master came to an abrupt halt in his harangue.

For Lad was cantering gleefully toward him, carrying something dark and heavy between his jaws. Straight to the Master came Lad. Carefully, at the Master's feet, he laid the rusty pistol.

Then, stepping back a pace, he looked up, eagerly, into the dumfounded man's face, tail waving, dark eyes aglint with expectation. It had been hard to locate the weapon, in all that tangle of lilac-stems. It had been harder to carry the awkwardly heavy thing all the way back, in his mouth, without dropping it. But, if this was the plaything the Master had chosen, Lad was only too willing to continue the game.

A little choking sound made the collie shift his gaze suddenly to the Mistress's troubled face. And the light of fun in his eyes was quenched. The sight of her splendid dog retrieving so joyously the weapon designed for his death, was almost too much for the Mistress's self-control.

The effect on the Master was different.

As Wefers made as though to jump forward and grab the pistol, the Master said sharply:

"*Watch* it, Laddie!"

Instantly, Lad was on the alert. The game, it seemed, had begun again, and along sterner lines. He was to guard this plaything;—particularly from the bearded intruder who was snatching so avidly for it.

There was a sharp growl, a flash of fierce white teeth, a bound. One of Lad's snowy little forepaws was on the fallen pistol. And the rest of Lad's sinewy body was crouching above it, fangs aglint, eyes blazing with hot menace.

Wefers jerked back his protruding arm, with extreme quickness; barely avoiding a deep slash from the collie's shearing eye-teeth. And Lad, continued to "watch" the pistol.

The dog was having a lovely time. Seldom had he been happier. All good collies respond in semi-psychic fashion to the moods of their masters. And, to Lad, the very atmosphere about him was thrilling just now to waves of stark excitement. With the delightful vanity which is a part of the collie make-up, he realized that in some manner he himself was a prominent part of this excitement. And he reveled in it.

As Wefers pulled back his imperiled arm, the Mistress stepped forward, before the Master could speak or move.

"Even if it were true that he could get rabies by a bite from a rabid dog," said she, "and even if that dog, yesterday, were mad, that wouldn't affect Laddie. For he didn't bite Laddie. He never got the chance. Lad pinned him to the ground. And while the mongrel was struggling to get up, you shot him. One of your bullets flicked Lad's foreleg. But the mongrel's teeth never came within twelve inches of him. I can testify to that."

"He was fighting with a mad dog!" reiterated Wefers, fumingly. "I saw 'em, myself. And when a dog is fighting, he's bound to get bit. I'm not here to argue over it. I'm here to enforce the law of the sov'r'n State of Noo Jersey, County of P'saic, Township of—"

"But the law declares a prisoner innocent, till he's proved guilty," urged the Mistress, restraining the Master, by a light hand on his restless arm. "And Lad's not been proved guilty. It isn't proved he was bitten, at all. I can testify he wasn't. My husband washed the scratch and he can tell you it wasn't made by a bite. Any veterinary can tell you the same thing, at a glance. We can establish the fact that Lad was not bitten. So even if the law lets you shoot a bitten dog,—which I don't believe it does,—it doesn't empower you to shoot Lad. Why!" she went on, shuddering slightly, "if Lad hadn't sprung between that brute and myself, you'd probably be wanting to shoot *me!* For I'd have been bitten, terribly, if Lad hadn't—"

"I'm not here to listen to silly nonsense!" announced Wefer, glaring at the watchful dog and back at the man and woman, "I came here in p'soot of my sworn dooty. I been balked and resisted by the two of you; and my pistol's been stole from me and a savage dog's been pract'c'lly sicked onto me. I'm an of'cer of the law. And I'm going to have the law on both of you, for int'fering with me like you have. And I'm going to get a court order to shoot—"

"Then you haven't a court order or any other authority to shoot him?" the Master caught him up. "You admit that! You came over here, thinking you could bluff us into letting you do it, just because you happen to wear a tin badge! I thought so. Now, my pink-whiskered friend, you'll stop shouting and making faces; and you'll listen to me, a minute. You aren't the first officer who has exceeded his authority on the chance that people will think he's acting within his rights. This time the bluff fails. With no warrant or summons or other legal power to back him, a constable has no more right on my place than any negro trespasser. What you may or may not be able to persuade some magistrate to do about this, I don't know. But, for the present, you'll clear out. Get that? I've warned you, in the presence of a witness. If you know anything of law, you know that a landowner, after such warning, may eject a trespasser by force. Go. And keep going. That's all."

Wefers sputtered wordlessly, from time to time, during the

tirade. But before its end, he fell silent and began to fidget. He himself was none too well versed in the matter of his legal rights of intrusion. And, for the moment, he had no chance to execute his errand. Later, armed with a magistrate's order, he could pay back with interest his humiliation of this morning. In the meantime—

"Gimme my gun!" he demanded in grouchy surrender.

The Master stooped; picked up the pistol, and held it in both hands. Lad, all eagerness, stood dancingly waiting for him to throw it again. But it was not thrown. Instead, the Master "broke" the weapon; shaking the greasy cartridges out on to his own palm and then transferring them to his pockets.

"In case of accidents," he explained, pleasantly, as he handed the pistol back to its scowling owner. "And if you'll stop at the post-office, this afternoon, you'll find these shells in an envelope in your letter-box. Now, chase; unless you want Lad to escort you to your boat. Lad is fine at escorting undesirables off the Place. Want to see him perform?"

But Wefers did not answer. Snatching the impotent pistol and shoving it back into his coattail pocket, he strode lakeward, muttering lurid threats as he went.

The Mistress watched his lank figure on its way down the lawn to the dock.

"It's-it's *awful!*" she faltered, clutching at her husband's arm. "Oh, you don't suppose he can—can really get leave to shoot Laddie, do you?"

"I don't know," answered the Master, as uneasy as she. "A mad-dog scare has a way of throwing everybody into a fool panic. There's no knowing what some magistrate may let him do. But one thing is mighty certain," he reassured her. "If the whole National Guard of New Jersey comes here, with a truckload of shooting-warrants, they aren't going to get Laddie. I promise you that. I don't quite know how we are going to prevent it. But we're going to. That's a pledge. So you're not to worry."

As they talked they continued to watch the constable in his

clumping exit from the Place. Wefers reached the dock, and stamped out to its extreme end, where was moored the livery scow he had commandeered for his journey across the lake from the village.

A light wind was blowing. It had caught the scow's wide stern and had swung it out from the dock. Wefers unhooked the chain and dropped it clankingly into the bottom. Then, with ponderous uncertainty, he stepped from the dock's string-piece to the prow of his boat.

A whiff of breeze slapped the loosened scow, broadside on, and sent it drifting an inch or two away. As a result, Homer Wefers' large shoe-sole was planted on the edge of the prow, instead of its center. His sole was slippery from the dew of the lawn. The prow's edge was still more slippery, from having been the scene of a recent fish-cleaning.

The constable's gangling body strove in vain to hold any semblance of balance. His foot slid out from its precarious perch, pushing the boat farther into the lake. And the dignified officer flapped wildly in mid-air.

Not being built on a lighter-than-air principle, he failed to hold this undignified aerial pose for more than the tenth of a second. At the end of that time he plunged splashingly into the lake, at a depth of something like eight feet of water.

"Good!" applauded the Master, as the Mistress gasped aloud in not wholly sorrowful surprise and as Lad ambled gayly down the lawn for a closer view of this highly diverting sight. "Good! I hope he ruins every stitch he has on; and then gets rheumatism and tonsilitis. He—"

The Master's babbling jaw fell slack; and the pleased grin faded from his face.

Wefers had come to the surface, after his ducking. He was fully three yards beyond the dock and as far from his drifting scow. And he was doing all manner of sensational things with his lanky arms and legs and body. In brief, he was doing everything except swim.

It was this phenomenon which had wiped away the Master's grin of pure happiness.

Any man may fall into the water, and may present a most ludicrous spectacle in doing so. But, on the instant he comes to the surface, his very first motions will show whether or not he is a swimmer. It had not occurred to the Master that anyone reared in the North Jersey lake-country should not have at least enough knowledge of swimming to carry him a few yards. But, even as many sailors cannot swim a stroke, so many an inlander, born and brought up within sight of fresh water, has never taken the trouble to grasp the simplest rudiments of natation. And such a man, very evidently, was Homer Wefers, Township Head Constable.

His howl of crass panic was not needed to prove this to the Master. His every wild antic showed it. But that same terror-stricken screech was required to set forth the true situation to the one member of the trio who had learned from birth to judge by sound and by scent, rather than by mere sight.

With no good grace, the Master yanked off his own coat and waistcoat, and bent to unstrap his hiking boots. He did not relish the prospect of a wetting, for the mere sake of saving from death this atrocious trespasser. He knew the man could probably keep afloat for at least a minute longer. And he was not minded to shorten the period of fear by ripping off his own outer garments with any melodramatic haste.

As he undid the first boot-latchet, he felt the Mistress's tense fingers on his shoulder.

"Wait!" she exhorted

Astounded at this cold-blooded counsel from his tender-hearted wife, he looked up, and followed the direction of her eagerly pointing hand.

"Look!" she was exulting. "It'll all solve itself! See if it doesn't. Look! He can't shoot Laddie, after—after—"

The Master was barely in time to see Lad swirl along the dock with express-train speed and spring far out into the lake.

The dog struck water, a bare ten inches from Wefers' madly tossing head. The constable, in his crazy panic, flung both bony arms about the dog. And, man and collie together disappeared under the surface, in a swirl of churned foam.

The Mistress cried aloud, at this hideous turn her pretty plan had taken. The Master, one shoe off and one shoe on, hobbled at top pace toward the dock.

As he reached the foot of the lawn, Lad's head and shoulders came into view above the little whirlpool caused by the sinking bodies' suction. And, at the same moment, the convulsed features of Homer Wefers showed through the eddy. The man was thrashing and twisting in a way that turned the lake around him into a white maelstrom.

As the Master set foot on the dock he saw the Collie rush forward with an impetus that sent both shaggy mahogany shoulders far out of water. Striking with brilliant accuracy, the dog avoided Wefers' flailing arms and feet, and clinched his strong teeth into the back of the drowning man's collar.

Thus, Lad was safe from the blindly clinging arms and from a kick. He had chosen the one strategic hold; and he maintained it. A splashing of the unwieldy body made both heads vanish under water, for a bare half-second, as the Master poised himself on the string-piece for a dive. But the dive was not made.

For the heads reappeared. And now, whether from palsy of fright or from belated intelligence,—Wefers ceased his useless struggles; though not his strangled shrieks for help. The collie, calling on all his wiry power, struck out for the dock; keeping the man's face above water, and tugging at his soggy weight with a scientific strength that sent the two, slowly but steadily, shoreward.

After the few feet of the haul, Wefers went silent. Into his blankly affrighted face came a look of foolish bewilderment. The Master, remembering his wife's hint, and certain now of Lad's ability to complete the rescue, stood waiting on the string-piece. Once, for a second, Wefers' eyes met his; but they were averted in queer haste.

As Lad tugged his burden beneath the stringpiece, the Master bent down and gripped the sodden wet shoulders of the constable. One none-too-gentle heave, and Wefers was lying in a panting and dripping heap on the clean dock. Lad, relieved of his heavy load, swam leisurely around to shore. It had been a delightfully thrilling day, thus far, for the collie. But he was just a bit tired.

By the time the dazed constable was able to sit up and peer owlishly into the unloving faces of the Mistress and the Master, Lad had shaken himself thrice and was pattering across the dock toward the group. From the two humans, Wefers' gaze shifted to the oncoming dog. Then he glanced back at the sullen depths of lake water beyond the string-piece. Then he let his head sink on his chest. For perhaps a whole minute, he sat thus; his eyes shut, his breath still fast and hysterical.

Nobody spoke. The Mistress looked down at the drenched man. Then she winked at the equally silent Master, and laid a caressing little hand on Lad's wet head. At length, Wefers lifted his face and glowered at the trio. But, as his eye met Lad's quizzically interested gaze, he fidgeted.

"Well?" prompted the Master, "do you want those cartridges back?"

Wefers favored him with a scowl of utter dislike. Then, his eyes again averted, the wet man mumbled:

"I come over here today, to do my dooty.—Dogs that get bit by mad dogs had ought to be shot.—I come over here to do my dooty. Likewise, I done it.—I shot that dog of yours that got bit, yest'day."

"Huh?" ejaculated the Master.

"This dog here looks some like him," went on Wefers, sulkily. "But it ain't him. And I'll so report to the author'ties.—I done what I come to do. The case is closed. And-and-if you folks ever want to sell your dog, why,—well, I'll just go mortgage something and—and buy him off'n you!"

CHAPTER III

NO TRESPASSING!

There were four of them; two gaudily-clad damsels and two men. The men, in their own way, were attired as gloriously as the maidens they were escorting. The quartet added generously to the glowing beauty of the summer day.

Down the lake they came, in a canoe modestly scarlet except for a single broad purple stripe under the gunwale. The canoe's tones blended sweetly with the pink parasol and blue picture hat of one of the women.

Stolid and unshaven fishermen, in drab scows, along the canoe's route, looked up from their lines, in bovine wonder at the vision of loveliness which swept resonantly past them. For the quartet were warbling. They were also doing queer musical stunts which are fondly miscalled "close harmony."

Thus do they and their kind pay homage to a divine day on a fire-blue lake, amid the hush of the eternal hills. Lesser souls may find themselves speaking in few and low-pitched words, under the holy spell of such surroundings. But to loftier types of holiday-seekers, the benignant silences of the wilderness are put there by an all-wise Providence for the purpose of being fractured by any racket denoting care-free merriment;—the louder the merrier. There is nothing so racket-breeding as a perfect day amid perfect scenery.

The four revelers had paddled down into the lake, on a day's picnicking. They had come from far up the Ramapo river; beyond Suffern. And the long downstream jaunt had made them hungry. Wherefore, as they reached mid-lakes they began to inspect the wooded shores for an attractive luncheon-site. And they found what they sought.

A half-mile to southward, a gently rolling point of land pushed out into the lake. It was smooth-shaven and emerald-bright. It formed the lower end of a lawn; sloping gently downward, a hundred yards or more, from a gray old house which nestled happily among mighty oaks on a plateau at the low hill's summit.

The point (with its patch of beach-sand at the water's edge, and with comfortable shade from a lakeside tree or so), promised an ideal picnic-ground. The shaven grass not only offered fine possibilities for an after-luncheon snooze; but was the most convenient sort of place for the later strewing of greasy newspapers and Japanese napkins and wooden platters and crusts and chicken bones and the like.

Moreover, a severely plain "No Trespass" sign, at the lake-margin, would serve as ideal kindling for a jolly little camp-fire. There is always a zest in using trespass boards for picnic fires. Not only are they seasoned and painted in a way to cause quick ignition, but people laugh so appreciatively, when one tells, afterward, of the bit of jovial audacity.

Yes, this point was just the place for luncheon and for siesta. It might have been made to order. And by tacit consent the two paddlers sent their multi-chrome canoe sweeping toward it. Five minutes later, they had helped the girls ashore and were lifting out the lunch-basket and various newspaper parcels and the red-and-purple cushions.

With much laughter and a snatch or two of close harmony, the lunch was spread. One of the men picked out a place for the fire (against the trunk of a two-century oak; perhaps the millionth noble old tree to be threatened thus with death from care-free picnickers' fires) and the other man sauntered across to the trespass board to annex it for kindling.

Everything was so happy and so complete and everyone was having such a perfect time! Into such moments Fate loves best to toss Trouble. And, this day, Fate played true to form.

As the fire-maker's hand was laid on the trespass board, even as his inconsequential muscles were braced to rip it loose from its post,—a squeal from the girl in the blue picture hat and the Nile-green georgette waist, checked his mirthful activities.

Now, there was nothing remarkable in the fact that the chromatic lass had squealed. Indeed, she and her equally fair companion had been squealing at intervals, all morning. But there was nothing coquettish or gay about this particular squeal. It savored rather of a screech. In its shrill note was a tiny thread of terror. And the two men wheeled about, to look.

The blue-hatted girl had paused in her dainty labor of helping to spread out the lunch; in order to peep inquisitively up the slope toward the tree-framed house above. It might be fun, after eating, to stroll up there and squint in through the veranda windows; or,—if no one was at home, to gather an armful of the roses that clambered over one end of the porch.

During that brief exploratory glance, her eye had been caught by something moving through the woods beyond.

Behind the house, these woods ran up to the highroad, a furlong above. A driveway led twistingly down from the gate-lodge, to the house. Along this drive, was pacing a dog.

As the girl caught sight of him, the dog halted in his lazy stroll and stood eagerly erect, his nose upraised, his tulip ears pricked. Sound or scent, or both, had been arrested by some unusual presence. And he paused to verify the warning.

As he stood there, an instant, in the shade-flecked driveway, the girl saw he was a collie; massive, graceful, majestic; in the full strength of his early prime; his shaggy coat of burnished mahogany-and-snow glinting back the showers of sun-rays that filtered down through the leaves.

Before the watching girl could take further note of him, the dog's aspect of tense listening merged into certainty. With no further shadow of doubt as to direction, he set off at a sweeping run past the house and toward the point.

He ran with head down; and with tawny ruff abristle. There was something in his lithe gallop that was as ominous as it was beautiful. And, nervous at the great collie's approach, the girl squealed.

It had been a dull morning for Lad. The Mistress was in town for the day. The Master was shut up in his study, hard at work. And, for once, he had not remembered to call Lad to a resting place on the study rug; before closing the door on the outside world. Alone and bored, the collie had wandered into the woods; in quest of possible rabbits to chase or squirrels to tree. Finding the sport tame, he started homeward. Midway down the drive, his supersensitive nostrils caught the whiff of alien humans on the Place. At the same time, he heard the raucous gabbling of several voices. Though his near-sighted eyes did not yet show the intruders to him, yet scent and sound made it ridiculously easy for him to trace them.

From early puppyhood, Lad had been the official guardian of the Place. He knew the limits of its thirty acres; from lake to highroad; from boundary fence to boundary fence. He knew, too, that visitors must not be molested as long as they were on the driveway; but that no stranger might be allowed to cross the land, by any other route; or to trespass on lawn or oak-grove.

And now, apparently, strangers were holding some sort of unlicensed revelry, down on the point. His sense of smell told him that neither the Master nor anyone else belonging to the Place was with them. True watchdog indignation swelled up in Lad's heart. And he ran at top speed.

The girl's three companions, turning at sight of her gesturing hand, beheld a mahogany-and-white thunderbolt whizzing down the hundred-yard slope toward them.

It chanced that both the men had served long apprenticeship as dog-fanciers; and that both of them knew collies. Thus, no second look was needed. One glimpse of the silently charging Lad told them all they needed to know. Not in this way does a blatant or bluffing watchdog seek to shoo off trespassers. This giant collie, with his lowered head and glinting fangs and ruffling hackles, meant business. And the men acted accordingly.

"Run for it!" bellowed one of them; setting a splendid example by reaching the beached canoe at a single scrambling bound. The second man was no whit behind him. Between them, the canoe, at one shove, was launched. The first man grabbed one of the girls by the arm and propelled her into the wobbling craft; while the other shoved off. The remaining girl,—she of the azure headgear and the verdant waist,—slipped on the grassy bank, in her flight, and sat down very hard, at the water's edge. Already the canoe was six feet from shore; and both men were doing creditable acrobatic stunts to keep it from turning turtle.

"Stand perfec'ly still," one of them exhorted the damsel, as he saw with horror that she had been left ashore in the tumbling flight. "Stand still and don't holler! Keep your hands high. It's likely he won't bother you. These highbred collies are pretty gentle with women; but some of 'em are blue murder to strange men. He—"

The man swayed for balance. His fellow-hero had brought the canoe about, in an effort to smite with uplifted paddle at the oncoming dog without venturing too close to the danger-line.

In the same moment, Lad had gained the brink of the lake. Ignoring the panic-struck woman on the bank, he flashed past her and galloped, body-deep, into the water; toward the swaying canoe.

Here he paused. For Lad was anything but a fool. And, like other wise collies, he had sense enough to realize that a swimming dog is one of the most helpless creatures in the universe; when it comes to self-defense.

Ashore, or in water shallow enough to maneuver his powerful body, Lad could give excellent account of himself against any normal foe. But, beyond his depth, he would fall easy victim to the first well-aimed paddle-stroke. And he knew it. Thus, hesitant, his snarling teeth not two yards from the canoe, he stood growling in futile indignation at the cranky craft's crankier occupants.

The girl who remained on shore plucked up enough panic-courage to catch her gaudy pink parasol by the ferule and to swing its heavy handle with all her fear-driven strength at Lad's skull.

Luckily, the aim was as bad as it was vehement. The handle grazed the dog's shoulder, then struck the lake with a force that snapped the flimsy parasol in two. Whereat the girl shrieked aloud; and scuttled back as Lad spun around to face her.

But she might as well have spared herself the scream. She was in no danger. True, the collie had whirled to seek and resent this new source of attack. But, seeing only a yelling and retreating woman behind him, he contented himself with a menacing growl, and turned again toward the canoe.

One of the men, poising himself, had swung aloft his paddle. Now, with full strength, he brought down the edged blade at the dog's head.

But it is one thing to aim a blow, from a tilting canoe; and quite another to make that blow land in the spot aimed for.

The whizzing paddle-blade missed Lad, clean. Not only because the dog veered sharply aside as it descended, but because the canoe, under the jarring heave of the striker's body, proceeded to turn turtle.

Into the water plopped the two men. Into the water, with them, splashed their rescued companion. This gentle soul had not ceased screaming, from the time she was hauled aboard. But now, submergence cut short her cries. A second later, the lamentations recommenced; in higher if more liquid volume. For, the shore, at the point sloped very gradually out to deeper water. And immediately, she and the two men had regained their foothold.

There, chest deep the trio stood or staggered. And, there, between them and the beach, raged Lad. None of the three cared to risk wading shoreward, with such an obstacle between themselves and land. The girl on the bank added her quota of squalls to those of her semi-engulfed friend; and one of the men began to reach far under water for a rock to throw at the guard dog.

The first shrill cry had reached the Master, as he sat at work in his study. Down the slope he came running; and stopped in slack-jawed amaze at the tableau in front of him.

On the bank hopped and wriggled a woman in vivid garments,—a woman who waved a broken parasol and seemed to be practicing an Indian war-howl. Elbow deep in the placid waters of the lake floundered another woman almost as wonderfully attired as the first, and quite as vocal. On either side of her was a drenched and gesticulating man. In the background bobbed an upset canoe. Between the two disrupted factions of the happy picnic party stood Lad.

The collie had ceased to growl; and, with head on one side, was looking in eager inquiry at the Master. Lad had carried this watchdog exploit to a point where the next move was hard to figure out. He was glad the Master had arrived, to take charge of the situation. It seemed to call for human, rather than canine, solution. And Lad was profoundly interested as to the sequel. All of which showed as clearly in the collie's whimsically expressive face as ever it could have been set forth in print.

Both men began to talk at once; with lurid earnestness and vast wealth of gesture. So did the women.

There was no need. The Master, already, had caught sight of the half-spread lunch on the grass. And it was by no means his first or his tenth experience with trespassers. He understood. Snapping his fingers, to summon Lad to his side, he patted the dog's silken head; and strove not to laugh.

"And just as we was sitting down, peaceful, to eat, and not harming no one at all and minding our own business," came a fragment of one man's oration, above the clamor of the others, "that big dark-sable collie of yours came tearing down on us and—"

The triple opposition of outcry and complaint blurred the rest of his enraged whine. But the Master looked out at him in new interest. The man had used the term, "dark-sable collie"; which, by the way, was the technical phrase for Lad's coloring. Not one non-collie-man in a thousand would have known the meaning of the term; to say nothing of using it by instinct. The Master stared curiously at the floundering and sputtering speaker.

"Aren't you the manager of the Lochaber Collie Kennels, up at

Beauville?" he asked, speaking loud enough to be heard above the subsiding din. "I think I've seen you at Westminster and at some of the local shows. Higham is your name, isn't it?"

"Yes, it is," returned the kennel man, truculent, but surprised almost into civility. "And this is my assistant, Mister Rice. And these two young lady friends of ours are—Say!" he broke off, furiously, remembering his plight and swinging back to rage, as he began to wade shoreward. "We're going to have the law on you, friend! Your collie tackled us when we was peaceably-"

"When you were peaceably ignoring this trespass sign of mine?" finished the Master. "Don't forget that. If you didn't have these girls with you, I'd keep my hands off Lad's collar and let him hold you out in the lake till it freezes for the winter. As it is, one of you men can swim out for your canoe and tow it in; and then the rest of you can bundle aboard it and finish your picnic on somebody else's land."

"Well!" shrilled the wet damsel, striding shoreward like some sloppily overdressed Venus rising from the sea. "Well! I *must* say! Nice neighborly, hospitable way to treat poor unfortunate—!"

"Trespassers?" suggested the Master, as she groped for a climax word. "You're right. It is no way to treat a woman who has fallen into the lake; trespasser or not. If you and this other young lady care to go up to the kitchen, the maids will see that your clothes are dried; and they'll lend you other clothes to go home in. Lad won't hurt you. And in this hot weather you're in no danger of catching cold. While you're gone, Higham and Rice can get hold of the canoe and right it and bail it out. And, by the way, I want one of you two men to clear that litter of food and greasy paper off my lawn. Then—"

"Into the kitchen!" snorted the wet maid. "Into the *kitchen?* I'm a lady! I don't go into kitchens. I—"

"No?" queried the Master, trying once more not to laugh. "Well, my wife does. So does my mother. I spoke of the kitchen because it's the only room with a fire in it, in this weather. If you'd prefer the barn or—"

"I won't step one foot in your house!" declaimed the girl. "Nor yet I didn't come here to be insulted. You've gone and spoiled our whole day, you big brute! Boys, go get that canoe! We won't lower ourselves by staying another minute on his rotten land. Afterward, our lawyer'll see what's the penalty for treating us like this! Hurry up!"

Rice had clumped along shore until he found a dead branch washed up in a recent rainstorm. Wading back into deeper water he was just able to reach the gunwale of the drifting canoe with the forked end of the bough and, by careful jockeying, to haul it within hand-grasp.

Aided by Higham, he drew the overturned craft to the beach and righted it. All the time, both men maintained a half-coherent diatribe, whose language waxed hotter and hotter and whose thunderbolts centered about the Master and his dog;—particularly about Lad;—and about the dire legal penalties which were to be inflicted on them.

The Master, still holding Lad's ruff, stood to one side during the work of salvaging the canoe; and while Rice replaced the paddles and cushions in it. Only when the two women were helped sputteringly aboard did he interfere.

"One minute!" he said. "I think you've forgotten your lunch. That and the ream or two of newspapers you've strewn around: and a few wooden dishes. I—"

"I picked up all the lunch that was worth saving," grunted Rice. "Your mangy collie trampled the rest of it, when he ran down here at us. I wisht it'd had strychnia in it and he'd et it! We'll go eat our dinner over to the village. And, before we go, I got this much more to say to *you*:—If—"

"Before you go," interrupted the Master, shifting himself and Lad between Higham and the canoe, "before you go, let me remind you that you've left a lot of litter on my clean lawn; and that I asked you to clean it up."

"Go clean it up, yourself!" snapped Rice, from the boat. "This upstage talk about 'trespassing' makes me sick! As soon as a guy has a three-dollar patch of bum land (with a mortgage eating it up, most likely), he always blats about 'trespassing' whenever decent folks happens to walk on it. Go clean up the papers, yourself! We ain't your slaves. You're due to hear a lot from us, later, too. Clean it, yourself!"

The ladies applauded these stirring proletariat sentiments right vigorously. But Higham did not applaud. Rice and the women were in the canoe. Higham had gone back to the picnic site for an overlooked cushion. On returning toward the beach, he had found the Master and Lad standing in his way. Loftily, he made as though to skirt them and reach the canoe.

"*Watch* him, Laddie!" whispered the Master, loosing his hold on the dog's ruff.

This, in the midst of Rice's tirade. Higham stood extremely still. As the others applauded, he began, very fervently, to swear.

"Higham," suggested the Master, "I've no personal objection to your blasphemy. If the women of your party can stand it, I can. But aren't you wasting a good deal of time! These papers have all got to be picked up, you know; and the camp nicely policed. Get busy."

Higham glowered on him in murderous hate; then at the tensely watching dog. Lad's upper lip curled. The man took a tentative step toward the beach. Lad crouched, panther-like; and a low growl parted still further his writhing lips.

Higham was enough of a collie man to foresee the inevitable next move. He stood stock still. The Master put his hand once more on Lad's ruff; but none too tightly. And he nodded toward the clutter of newspapers and wooden plates. Higham's language soared spoutingly to high heaven. But he turned back and, with vicious grabs, cleared the lawn of its unsightly litter.

"Take it into the boat with you." said the Master. "That's all. Goodbye. See you at the Beauville show."

Waiting only for the canoe and its four vociferous occupants to start safely from shore, the Master returned to the house; Lad at his heels; pursued by a quadruple avalanche of abuse from the damp trespassers.

"There'll be a comeback of some kind to this, Laddie," he told the collie, as they moved on. "I don't know just what it'll be. But those two worthy youths didn't look at all lovingly at us. And there's nothing else in country life so filthily mean as an evicted trespasser. Don't let's say anything to the Mistress about it, Lad. It'd only worry her! And—and she'll think I ought to have invited all those panhandlers up to the house to get dry. Perhaps she'd be right, too. She generally is."

A week later, Lad received a summons that made his heart sink. For he knew precisely what it foretold. He was called to the bathroom; where awaited him a tub half full of warm water.

Now, baths were no novelty to Lad. But when a bath tub contained certain ingredients from boxes on the dog-closet shelf,—ingredients that fluff the coat and burnish it and make all its hairs stand out like a Circassian Beauty's, that meant but one thing.

It meant a dog-show was at hand.

And Lad loathed dog-shows, as he loathed tramps and castor oil and motorcycles.

After a single experience, he had never been taken to one of those canine ordeals known as "three-or-more-day shows." But the Mistress and the Master rejoiced at his triumphs at such local one-day shows as were within pleasant driving distance of the Place. These exhibitions entailed no great strain or danger. Lad's chief objection to them was that he hated to be chirped to and pawed and stared upon by an army of strangers.

Such a one-day event was the outdoor Charity Dogshow at the Beauville Country Club, forty miles to northeast of the Place; an easy two-hour drive. It was to be a "specialty show"; at which the richness and variety of prizes were expected to atone for the lack of A. K. C. points involved.

A premium-list of the show had been mailed to the Place; and one of its "specials" had caught the Mistress's quick eye and quicker imagination. The special was offered by Angus McGilead, an exiled

Scot whose life fad was the Collie; and whose chief grievance was that most American breeders did not seem able to produce collies with the unbelievable wealth of outer-and-undercoat displayed by the oversea dogs. This particular special was offered in the following terms:

Embossed Sterling Silver Cup,
9 Inches High (Genuine Antique)
For The Best-Coated Collie Shown.

Now, Lad's coat was the pride of the Mistress's heart. By daily brushings she kept it in perfect condition and encouraged its luxuriant growth. When she read of McGilead's eccentric offer, she fell to visualizing the "embossed sterling silver cup, 9 inches high (genuine antique)" as it would loom up from the hedge of dog-show prizes already adorning the living room trophy-shelves.

Summer is the zero hour for collies' coats. Yet, this year, Lad had not yet begun to shed his winter raiment; and he was still in full bloom. This fact decided the Mistress. Not one collie in ten would be in anything like perfect coat. And the prize cup grew clearer and nearer, to her mental vision. Hence the series of special baths and brushings. Hence, too, Laddie's daily-increasing gloom.

At eight o'clock on the morning of the show, the Mistress and the Master, with Lad stretched forlornly on the rear seat of the car, set forth up the Valley on the forty-mile run to Beauville. On the tonneau floor, in front of Lad, rested a battered suitcase, which held his toilet appurtenances;—brushes, comb, talcum, French chalk, show-leash, sponge, crash towel, squeaking rubber doll (this to attract his bored interest in the ring and make him "show") and a box of liver cut in small bits and fried stiff.

Lad blinked down at the suitcase in morose disapproval. He hated that bag. It spelt "dogshow" to him. Even the presence of the delicious fried liver and of the mildly dramatic squeaking doll could not atone for the rest of its contents and for all they implied.

As the car sent the miles slipping behind and as the Mistress and the Master glanced back less and less often for a pat or a cheery word to their sulking chum, Lad's dislike for that pestilential bag grew sharper. True, it held squares of fried liver;—liver whose heavenly odor penetrated through the musty leather smell of the suitcase and to the dog's acute senses. Also, it held a doll which exuded thrilling squeaks when gently bitten. But these things, he knew full well, were designed as show-ring baits; not as free gifts.

No, the bag was his enemy. And, unlike his few other natural foes, Lad had never been bidden to leave it unmolested. This memory came to him, in the midst of his blues. He eyed the loathsome suitcase through quizzical half-shut eyes, as it rocked and careened at his feet with every jounce of the car. And into his brain shot the devil of mischief.

Bending down his shapely head, he took the handle of the case between his teeth. Then, bracing his little white forepaws on the slippery leather seat, he heaved with all the mighty strength of his back and shoulders. Under such urgence, the light suitcase swung high in air. A sideways toss of the muscular throat, and the suitcase whirled clear of the car door and of the running-board beneath. Then Lad let go; and settled himself back smugly in the seat. The luckless suitcase smote the road dust and rolled into a grassy ditch. The car sped on. Lad, for the moment, was nearly happy. If he were not able to dodge the show itself, at least he had gotten rid of the odious thing which held so much he detested and which was always an inseparable part of the ordeals he was taken to.

Arrived at the country club whose grounds had been fitted for the charity show, Lad was benched in the shade. And there, all the rest of the morning, he remained. For Loder, judge of the collies and Old English Sheepdogs and of two other breeds, had missed a train from Canada; and had not yet arrived. His various classes were held up, pending his advent.

"Loder's a lucky man, at that," commented the Toy Breeds judge, with whom the Master chanced to be talking. "And he'll be still luckier if he misses the whole show. You 'small exhibitors' have no notion of the rotten deal handed to a dog-show judge;—

though lots of you do more than your share toward making his life a burden. Before the judging begins, some of the exhibitors act as if they wanted to kiss him. Nothing's too good for him. He wades chin-deep through flattery and loving attentions. Then, after the judging is over, he is about as popular with those same exhibitors as a typhoid germ. No one can say bad enough things about him. He's 'incompetent,' he's 'a grafter,—'he's 'afraid of the big kennels,'—he's 'drunk.' He's any of these things; or all of them put together. Nobody's satisfied. Everybody has had a raw deal. Everybody's hammer is out for the poor slob of a judge. Well, not everybody's, of course. There are some real sportsmen left crawling on the surface of the earth. But the big majority pan him, all the way home; and then some of them roast him in print. The Income Tax man is a popular favorite, compared with a dog-show judge."

"But—"

"Then, again," pursued the Toy Breeds man, "he's got to leave his heart at home, if he doesn't want it to ache when he has to 'gate' the second-rate mutts shown by outsiders who never exhibited before and who think their pet dog ought to get every prize because he's so cunning and friendly. I hate to—"

The Mistress came hurrying up from a careful inspection of the line of collies. Drawing her husband aside, she whispered, excitedly:

"There's only one other collie here, whose coat can anywhere near equal Laddie's. The rest are all in shabby summer coat. Come across and let me show him to you. I'm—I'm afraid he has a gorgeous coat. Not that _I_ think it's half as good as Lad's," she added, loyally, as she piloted the Master between the double lines of clamorous dogs. "But—oh, I'm so afraid the judge may think it is! You see, he doesn't know Laddie as we do."

She stopped before a bench whereon lay a pale golden sable collie; almost corn-colored; who boasted a wealth and magnificence of coat that made the Master open his eyes wide.

The dog was smaller and slighter of frame than was Lad. Nor, in head and expression, was he Lad's equal. But his coat was every bit as luxuriant. Indeed, there was perhaps a shade more of it than Lad carried.

A collie's coat, as a rule, takes about seven months to grow. Thus, each year, it comes into full bloom a little later than on the year before. And, in course of time, it is prone to reach its climax of excellence in summer. This was the lot of both Lad and the paler-hued dog.

"Lochaber King," read the Master, from his catalog. "H'm! That's Colonel Osbourne's greatest pup. Remember, we saw him at Westminster? It's nip-and-tuck, between him and Lad; with a little in this dog's favor. Tough luck!"

"Oh, this has been just one of those days nobody wants!" mourned the Mistress. "First, our forgetting to bring along Laddie's suitcase, though I could have sworn I saw you lift it aboard,—and then the judge not being here; and now this horrid collie with his wonderful coat! What next, I wonder?"

Like a well-staged bit of mechanism, the reply to her rhetorical question came down to her from heaven. It came in the shape of a thunder-roll that began far off and reverberated from mountain to mountain; then muttered itself into silence in the more distant hills. The Mistress, like everyone else, looked skyward.

The hazy blue of the summer noon was paling to dirty gray and black. Up from the Hudson, a fast-mounting array of dun and flame-shot clouds were butting their bullying way. No weather-prophet was needed to tell these hillcountry folk that they were in for a thunderstorm;—and for what one kennel-man described as "a reg'lar ol' he-one," at that.

Now, under right conditions, an open-air dogshow is a thing of beauty and of joy. At such places as Tuxedo and one or two others it is a sight to be remembered. But in rainy weather,—especially in a tumultuous thunderstorm, it has not one redeeming feature.

The Beauville Show Committee,—like all experts in such matters, had taken this chance into account. Down the aisles of benches and through the questioning and scared groups of exhibitors ran attendants and officials; shouting that the Country Club polo stables and the wide spaces under the clubhouse verandas had been fitted up for emergency quarters, where the dogs might be housed, dry and safe, until the passing of the storm.

Up to the Master hurried a club page-boy.

"This way, sir!" he panted. "I saved a special box stall, in the first stable, for your collie."

"*You* saved it?" queried the puzzled Master, while the Mistress began to unfasten Lad's leash. "How did you happen to do that?"

"I was told to, sir," answered the boy. "A—a gentleman told me to, just now. One of the of'cers of the club. I don't know his name. He showed me the stall; and he told me to take your dog there."

"That's mighty, decent; whoever did it," said the Master, whistling the freed dog to him and setting forth in the boy's wake, toward the welcoming stables. "I wish you knew his name. I'd like to thank him."

The stable was dim-lit, at best. Now, the gathering storm made it as dark as twilight. The box stall to which Lad was led was almost pitch black; its shuttered window being closed. Still, it was shelter. Leaving the Master and the Mistress to consign Lad to his new quarters, the boy scuttled of to a harness-room. There, an eagerly-questioning man was awaiting him.

"Yep," broke in the boy, through a volley of inquiries. "I done it, all right, all right, Mr. Higham. They're moorin' him in Stall Five, right now. How about those two soft dollars? Hey?"

"You earned 'em, O. K.," grinned Higham. "Here you are. Two,—count 'em, two. And now, chase along, sonny. I'm busy."

He turned to a large bowl in which he had been mixing the contents of three or four bottles. And the boy saw his fingers were fiery red.

"What's the matter?" demanded the youngster, in high excitement. "That's blood, ain't it?"

"No," denied Higham. "Blood's light red. This is crimson. Remember the time we run in that joke on Daddy Price, by dipping his prize white leghorns in crimson dye, just before the Madison Square Garden Poultry Show? Well, this is the same stuff."

"Do I remember it?" snickered the boy. "He was ragin', for fair. Couldn't get it off, to save him. It stayed, that color, on 'em, till they'd shed the last one of last year's crop of feathers. Sure, I remember. Why wouldn't I? Didn't I git a dollar for holdin' 'em for you? And another dollar for keepin' my mouth shut? But what are you lottin' to do with the stuff, this time? No chickens here; or—"

"Nope," assented Higham. "No chickens here. Hold on, a second!"

He stood, musing. Then he spoke.

"I was going to play a lone hand, on this," he said, presently. "I didn't even dare let Rice in on it. He'd be dead-sure to tell that gabby girl he's going to marry. And it'd get all over the country in a week. And that'd lose me my job, if the boss heard of it. I was going to play it alone. That's why I left Rice and Willett to put up the dogs for me. But,—I'm blest if I know how I'm to hold him and dye him at the same time. He's as strong as an ox. You—you're a good, close-tongued kid, Harry. You kept your mouth shut about Price's chickens. Could you keep it shut,—for another dollar,— about this? If you'll do that, and lend me a hand—How about it?"

"What's the main idea?" asked the boy, much intrigued by the beauty of the dye on Higham's fingers; and squirming with embarrassed self-importance at the man's flattering tone. "I'll help out, all right. Only,—"

"Here's the notion," said Higham, coming out of momentary self-communion. "And if you ever spill it, your mail will be sent to you at the hosp't'l, for a spell. You saw that big dark sable collie I had you steer into Stall Five? It cost me another two dollars to get Abrams to let me have the use of that stall. The idea come to me, in a jolt, first crack of thunder I heard. Well, I'm due to 'get' that dog and the mucker who owns him, too. Them and I had a run-in, once; and I been honing for a chance to square things, ever since. I've seen 'em at shows and I've asked folks about 'em, too.

He sets more store by that dog than he'd set by most humans. He's pleased as Punch, every time the collie hauls down a cup at one of these neighborhood shows. Well, that dog ain't going to be fit to go to another show, for a year. He ain't going to be fit to look at, for that long. He's going to be a laughing stock. His owners won't brag any more about him, neither. They'll be glad enough to keep him out of sight."

The boy, listening with ever-widening eyes, chanced to shift his gaze to the big bowl of new-mixed dye. And a light broke on him.

"You—you're aimin' to soak him with that stuff?" he whispered, in awe at such combined courage and genius.

"Uh-uh," assented Higham. "I don't know what color the crimson stuff will turn the dark part of his coat. But whatever color it is, it'll be as funny as a box of three-tailed snakes. I've put a glass of ammonia into the dye, to make it 'set' quicker. It—"

"Gee, but you're a wonder!" sighed the worshiping boy. "D'ye s'pose I'll ever git to be as smart as you are?"

"It all depends on how you make use of your brains," returned Higham, complacently. "But I was some smarter than you to begin with. I—"

"But—"

Higham went on, more briskly:

"I've got this bag to put over his head when I open the stall door. That'll put him out of the biting business, till it's peeled away from his jaws, after he's got a real good rubbing. But he'll likely wriggle, a lot. And I'll need you to sit on his head. Likewise to carry this bowl and the sponge, while I'm opening the door and getting the bag over his head. Are you game?"

"I sure am!" breathed the enraptured boy.

"Come 'long, then. The stuff's ready; and we don't want to waste any time. Go ahead and see if there's anyone in that end of the stable." Two minutes later, the pair groped their way through the dense gloom, to Stall Five. They walked with exaggerated care; though the roar of the storm would have deadened the sound of a cavalry charge. Handing over the bowl and sponge to his assistant, Higham produced from under his coat a thick burlap bag with a drawstring at its neck. Then, he opened the door of the box stall, a few inches and stared in.

By straining his eyes, he could just see the vague outline of the big collie. The dog arose from a bundle of straw, stretched himself fore and aft, and walked gravely forward to welcome the visitors who were so kindly easing his loneliness. He was barely visible, in the dimness.

But there was light enough for Higham's purpose. With practiced hand, he shoved the bag over the beautiful silken head, as the collie stepped majestically toward him. Then, deftly, he threw the indignant and struggling dog to the floor, and bade the boy come in; and shut the gate behind him.

With the passing of another hour, the rain ceased; and a glory of afternoon sunlight bathed the freshened world. At about the same time, the belated collie judge arrived at the clubhouse. Word was sent forth that all dogs were to be returned to their benches and that the judging of the collies and of certain other breeds would begin at once.

There was a general hustle and confusion, as exhibitors led forth their dogs from shelter; benching them and plying brush and chalk and towel in frantic haste.

Higham summoned Rice and another of the kennel men and bade them bring forth the Lochaber dogs. Instead of helping them with his task, Higham himself ran to the top of the clubhouse steps, from which he could survey not only the benches but also the stables and the lawn between. There, quivering with hard-held excitement, he stood; with the air of one who has chosen a grandstand seat for some thrilling event. He wore a pair of thick gloves. As he had discarded the linen duster which he had worn during the dyeing process, there was no betraying splash of color on his severely correct garb.

People were trooping out from the shelter of the clubhouse.

With half an eye, Higham observed these; chuckling at thought of the everincreasing number of spectators to his rare comedy. Of a sudden, the chuckle changed to a gasp.

Out through the doorway, and onto the veranda, strolled Colonel Osbourne, owner of the Lochaber Collie Kennels. With him walked the Mistress and the Master.

At the Mistress's side paced Lad.

"It was so careless of us to leave the suitcase at home!" the Mistress was saying. "I don't know how we could have groomed him, Colonel, if you hadn't come to our rescue by turning that kit bag's heaven-sent contents over to us. Besides, it gave us the excuse to bring Laddie up into the house; instead of leaving him all alone in that black stall. He hates thunderstorms, and—"

A yell, from somewhere, interrupted her. The yell was caught up. It merged into a multiple roar of inextinguishable laughter. The Mistress saw a hundred faces all turned in one direction, The faces were convulsed with mirth. A hundred derisively wondering fingers were pointing. She ran to the veranda rail and looked down.

Across the patch of greensward, from the stables, a man and a dog were advancing. The man was shaking his fist at the world at large and fairly dancing with rage.

But it was the dog, and not he, that caused the Homeric gusts of merriment and the gobbling chorus of amazed questions. The dog was a collie; noble of aspect, massive of coat.

But that same coat vied with the setting sun in garish brilliancy of hue. Never since the birth of time, had such a beast been seen by mortals. From the tip of his aristocratic nose to the plume of his sweeping tail, the collie was one blazingly vivid mass of crimson! He fairly irradiated flaring red lights. His coat was wet and it hung stickily to his lean sides, as if he had just come from a swim. And it was tinted like a chromo of a prairie fire.

Following more slowly to the veranda's edge, Colonel Osbourne had begun a reply to the Mistress's half-finished speech of gratitude for his hospitality.

"I was only too glad to be of service," said he. "That's a grand dog you have. It was a real pleasure to help in his grooming. Besides, I profited by it. You see, my Lochaber King was quartered in a muddy corner under the veranda. So I took the liberty of telling my man, Rice, to put him in that comfortable big stall of Lad's. I am the chief gainer by the—"

His courtly speech became a gurgle of horror. For, his eyes fell on the ragingly advancing Rice. And, by deduction, he recognized the crimson monstrosity at Rice's heels as his beloved Lochaber King.

Before the apoplectic Colonel could speak, Lad created a diversion on his own account. He had been sniffing the air, reminiscently, for a few seconds. Now, his eyes verified what his nostrils had told him. A pallidly glaring and shaking man, leaning against the veranda rail for support, had an oddly familiar scent and appearance to Laddie.

The collie stepped forward to investigate. The nerve-smashed Higham saw him coming; and thrust out one gloved hand in frightened rebuff.

The flicking gesture was unpleasantly like a blow. As the menacing hand slapped toward his jaws, Lad caught at it, in wary self-defense.

He recalled this man, now. He remembered he had been bidden to "watch" him. He did not spring at his assailant. But a warning snap answered the frenzied thrust of the hand. His teeth closed lightly on the glove-fingers, just as Higham, in fear, jerked back his arm.

The loose glove came away in the dog's mouth.

Colonel Osbourne, wheeling about to demand some explanation of his kennel-manager, beheld a bare hand as vividly crimson as Lochaber King's ruined coat.

"Laddie," observed the Mistress, that evening, as she placed on the top trophy-shelf an embossed silver cup, antique, and nine inches high, and stood back pride fully, to note the effect. "Laddie, I know—I just *know*,—you'd have won it, even if poor Lochaber King had competed. But,—oh, I wish I could make head or tail of any of the things that have happened, today! How do you suppose it all started, anyhow, dear?" she asked, turning to her husband for help in the riddle.

"I'd be willing to bet a year's pay it 'all started' about six feet from shore in this lake," responded the Master, "and about a fortnight ago."

But he spoke it in the depths of his own guiltily exultant heart. Outwardly, he merely grinned; and said with vacuous conviction:

"Laddie, you're a grand dog. And,—if you didn't win that cup from Lochaber King in one way, you certainly won it in another!"

CHAPTER IV.
HERO-STUFF

Life was monstrous pleasant, for Lad, at the Place. And never, except in early puppyhood, was he lonely. Never until the Master was so foolish as to decide in his own shallow human mind that the big collie would be happier with another collie for comrade and mate.

After that, loneliness more than once crept into Laddie's serene life; and into the dark sorrowful eyes behind which lurked a soul. For, until one has known and relied on the companionship of one's kind, there can be no loneliness.

The Master made another blunder—this one on his own account and on the Mistress's,—when he bought a second collie, to share Lad's realm of forest and lawn and lake. For, it is always a mistake to own two dogs at a time. A single dog is one's chum and guard and worshiper. If he be rightly treated and talked to and taught, he becomes all-but human. Because he is forced to rely solely on humans, for everything. And his mind and heart respond to this. There is no divided allegiance.

One dog in a home is worth ten times as much to his owners, in every way, as are two or more dogs. Especially if the one dog be such a collie as Sunnybank Lad. This the Master was due to discover.

On a sloppy and drippy and muggy afternoon, late in October,— one of those days nobody wants,—the Master came home from town; his fall overcoat showing a decided list to starboard in the shape of an egregiously bulged side-pocket.

The Mistress and Lad, as ever, came forth to greet the returning man. Lad, with the gayly trumpeting bark which always he reserved for the Mistress or the Master after an absence of any length, cavorted rapturously up to his deity. But, midway in his welcoming advance, he checked himself; sniffing the sodden October air, and seeking to locate a new and highly interesting scent which had just assailed his sensitive nostrils.

The Master put an end to the mystery, forthwith, by reaching deep into his overcoat's swollen pocket and fishing out a grayish golden ball of squirming fluff.

This handful of liveliness he set gingerly on the veranda floor; where it revealed itself as an eight-weeks old collie pup.

"Her name is 'Lady,'" expounded the Master, as he and the Mistress gazed interestedly down upon the sprawling and wiggling puppy. "Her pedigree reads like a page in Burke's Peerage. She—"

He paused. For Lad had moved forward to where the infant collie was trying valiantly to walk on the slippery boards. The big dog regarded the puppy; his head on one side, his tulip ears cocked; his deep-set eyes friendly curious. This was Lad's first experience with one of the young of his species. And he was a bit puzzled; albeit vastly interested.

Experimentally, he laid one of his tiny white forepaws lightly on the mite's fuzzy shoulder. Instantly, the puppy growled a falsetto warning to him to keep his distance. Lad's plumed tail began to wag at this sign of spirit in the pigmy. And, with his curved pink ribbon of tongue, he essayed to lick the shivering Lady. A second growl rewarded this attention. And Lady sought to avoid further contact with the shaggy giant, by scrambling at top speed to the edge of the veranda.

She miscalculated the distance or else her nearsighted baby eyes failed to take account of the four-foot drop to the gravel drive below. Too late, she tried to check her awkward rush. And, for a moment, her fat little body swayed perilously on the brink.

The Mistress and the Master were too far away to catch her in time to prevent a fall which might well have entailed a broken rib or a wrenched shoulder. But Lad was nearer. Also, he moved faster.

With the speed of lightning, he made a dive for the tumbling Lady. As tenderly as if he were picking up a ball of needles, he caught her by the scruff of the neck, lifting her in the air and depositing her at the Mistress's feet.

The puppy repaid this life-saving exploit by growling still more wrathfully and by snapping in helpless menace at the big dog's nose. But Lad was in no wise offended. Deaf to the praise of the Mistress,—a praise which ordinarily threw him into transports of embarrassed delight,—he stood over the rescued pup; every inch of his magnificent body vibrant with homage and protectiveness.

From that hour, Lad was the adoring slave of Lady.

He watched over her, in her increasingly active rambles about the Place. Always, on the advent of doubtful strangers, he interposed his own furry bulk between her and possible kidnaping. He stood beside her as she lapped her bread-and-milk or as she chewed laboriously at her fragment of dog-biscuit.

At such times, he proved himself the mortal foe of Peter Grimm, the Mistress's temperamental gray kitten, with whom he was ordinarily on very comfortable terms. Peter Grimm was the one creature on the Place whom Lady feared. On the day after her arrival, she essayed to worry the haughty catkin. And, a second later, the puppy was nursing a brace of deep red scratches at the tip of her inquiring black nostrils.

Thereafter, she gave Peter Grimm a wide berth. And the cat was wont to take advantage of this dread by making forays on Lady's supper dish. But, ever, Lad would swoop down upon the marauder, as Lady cowered whimperingly back on her haunches; and would harry the indignant cat up the nearest tree; herding her there until Lady had licked the dish clean.

Lad went further, in his fealty to the puppy. Sacrificing his own regal dignity, he would romp with her, at times when it would have been far more comfortable to drowse. He bore, without murmur, her growling assaults on his food; amusedly standing aside while she annexed his supper's choicest bits.

He endured, too, her occasional flurries of hot temper; and made no protest when Lady chose to wreak some grievance against life by flying at him with bristling ruff and jaws asnarl. Her keen little milk teeth hurt like the mischief, when they dug into his ears or his paws, in one of these rage-gusts. But he did not resent the pain or the indignity by so much as drawing back out of harm's way. And, afterward, when quick repentance replaced anger and she strove to make friends with him again, Lad was inordinately happy.

To both the Mistress and the Master, from the very outset, it was plain that Lady was not in any way such a dog as their beloved Lad. She was as temperamental as Peter Grimm himself. She had hair-trigger nerves, a swirlingly uncertain temper that was scarce atoned for by her charm and lovableness; and she lacked Lad's stanchness and elusive semi-human quality. The two were as different in nature as it is possible for a couple of well-brought-up thoroughbred collies to be. And the humans' hearts did not go out to Lady as to Lad. Still, she was an ideal pet, in many ways. And, Lad's utter devotion to her was a full set of credentials, by itself.

Autumn froze into winter. The trees turned into naked black ghosts; or, rather, into many-stringed harps whereon the northwest gales alternately shrieked and roared. The fire-blue lake was a sheet of leaden ice, twenty inches thick. The fields showed sere and grayly lifeless in the patches between sodden snow-swathes. Nature had flown south, with the birds; leaving the northern world a lifeless and empty husk, as deserted as last summer's robin-nests.

Lady, in these drear months of a dead world, changed as rapidly as had the smiling Place. From a shapeless gray-gold fuzzy baby, she grew lank and leggy. The indeterminate fuzz was buried under a shimmering gold-and-white coat of much beauty. The muskrat face lengthened and grew delicately graceful, with its long muzzle and exquisite profile.

Lady was emerging from clownish puppyhood into the charm of youth. By the time the first anemones carried God's message of spring through the forests' lingering snow-pall, she had lost her adolescent gawkiness and was a slenderly beautiful young collie; small and light of bone, as she remained to the day of her death, but with a slimness which carried with it a hint of lithe power and speed and endurance.

It was in the early spring that the Master promoted Lady from her winter sleeping-quarters in the tool-house; and began to let her spend more and more time indoors.

Lady had all the promise of becoming a perfect housedog. Fastidious, quick to learn, she adapted herself almost at once to indoor life. And Lad was overjoyed at her admission to the domain where until now he had ruled alone. Personally, and with the gravity of an old-world host, he conducted her from room to room. He even offered her a snoozing-place in his cherished "cave," under the piano, in the music room the spot of all others dearest to him.

But it was dim and cheerless, under the piano; or so Lady seemed to think. And she would not go there for an instant. She preferred the disreputable grizzly-bear rug in front of the living room hearth. And, temporarily deserting his loved cave, Lad used to lie on this rug at her side; well content when she edged him off its downy center and onto the bumpy edges.

All winter, Lady's sleeping quarters had been the tool-house in the back garden, behind the stables. Here, on a sweet-smelling (and flea-averting) bed of cedar shavings, she had been comfortable and wholly satisfied. But, at once, on her promotion, she appeared to look upon the once-homelike tool-house as a newly rich daylaborer might regard the tumbledown shack where he had spent the days of his poverty.

She avoided the tool-house; and even made wide detours to avoid passing close to it. There is no more thoroughgoing snob, in certain ways, than a high-bred dog. And, to Lady, the tool-house evidently represented a humiliating phase of her outlived past.

Yet, she was foredoomed to go back to the loathed abode. And her return befell in this way:

In the Master's study was something which Lady considered the most enthrallingly wonderful object on earth. This was a stuffed American eagle; mounted, rampant and with outflung wings, on a papier-mache stump.

Why the eagle should have fascinated Lady more than did the leopard-or-bear rugs or other chase-trophies, in the various downstairs rooms, only Lady herself could have told. But she could not keep her eyes off of it. Tiptoeing to the study door, she used to stand for half an hour at a time staring at the giant bird.

Once, in a moment of audacity, she made a playful little rush at it. Before the Master could intervene, Lad had dashed between her and the sacred trophy; and had shouldered her gently but with much firmness out of the room; disregarding her little swirl of temper at the interference.

The Master called her back into the study. Taking her up to the eagle, he pointed at it, and said, with slow emphasis:

"Lady! Let it *alone!* Let—it—*alone!*"

She understood. For, from babyhood, she had learned, by daily practice, to understand and interpret the human voice. Politely, she backed away from the alluring bird. Snarling slightly at Lad, as she passed him in the doorway, she stalked out of the room and went out on the veranda to sulk.

"I'm glad I happened to be here when she went for the eagle," said the Master, at lunch that day. "If I hadn't, she might have tackled it sometime, when nobody was around. And a good lively collie pup could put that bit of taxidermy out of commission in less than five seconds. She knows, now, she mustn't touch it."

He spoke smugly; his lore on the subject being bounded by his experiences in teaching Lad the simple Law of the Place. Lad was one of the rare dogs to whom a single command or prohibition was enough to fix a lesson in his uncannily wise brain for life. Lady was not. As the Master soon had occasion to learn.

Late one afternoon, a week afterward, the Mistress had set forth on a round of neighborhood calls. She had gone in the car; and had taken Lad along. The Master, being busy and abhorring calls, had stayed at home. He was at work in his study; and Lady was drowsing in the cool lower hall.

A few minutes before the Mistress was due to return for dinner, a whiff of acrid smoke was wafted to the man's nostrils.

Now, to every dweller in the country, there is one all-present peril; namely, fire. And, the fear of this is always lurking worriedly in the back of a rural householder's brain. A vagrant breath of smoke, in the night, is more potent to banish sleep and to start such a man to investigating his house and grounds than would be any and every other alarm known to mortals.

Even now, in broad daylight, the faint reek was enough to bring the Master's mind back to earth and the Master's body to its feet. Sniffing, he went out to find the cause of the smell. The chimneys and the roof and the windows of the house showing no sign of smoke, he explored farther; and presently located the odor's origin in a small brush-fire at some distance behind the stables. Two of the men were raking pruned vine-suckers and leaves onto the blaze. The wind set away from the house and stables. There was nothing to worry over. Ashamed of his own fussiness, the Master went back to his work.

As he passed the open study window, on his way indoors, a motion inside made him stop. He was just in time to see Lady trot into the room, crouch playfully, and then spring full at the stuffed eagle.

His shout deflected the young dog's leap, and kept her merrily outstretched jaws from closing on the bird. As it was, the impact knocked the eagle and the papier-mache stump to the floor; with much clatter and dust.

The Master vaulted in through the window; arriving on the study floor almost as soon as did the overthrown bird. Lady was slinking out into the hall; crestfallen and scared. The Master collared her and brought her back to the scene of her mischief.

The collie had disobeyed him. Flagrantly she had sinned in assailing the bird; after his injunction of "Let it alone!" There could be no doubt, from her wriggling aspect of guilt, that she knew she was doing wrong. Worse, she had taken sneaky advantage of his absence in order to spring at the eagle. And disgust warred with the Master's normal indignation.

Speaking as quietly as he could bring himself to speak, he told Lady what she had done and what a rotten thing it had been. As he talked to the utterly crestfallen pup, he was ransacking a drawer of his desk in search of a dogwhip he had put there long ago and had never had occasion to use.

Presently, he found it. Pointing to the overthrown trophy, he brought the lash down across the shrinking collie's loins. He did not strike hard. But he struck half a dozen times; and with glum knowledge that it was the only course to take.

Never before in her eight foolish months of life, had Lady known the meaning of a blow. While the whip-slashes were too light to do more than sting her well-mattressed back, yet the humiliation of them seared deep into her sensitive nature. No sound did she utter. But she cowered flat to the floor; and trembled as if in a hard chill.

The whipping was over, in a few seconds. Again the Master explained to her what it had been inflicted for. Then, calling her to follow, he led the way out of doors and toward the stables. Stomach to earth, the shamed and miserable Lady writhed along, close at his heels.

The Master passed the stables and walked toward the brush fire, where the two men were still at work. But he did not go within a hundred feet of the fire. Turning, after he had left the stables behind him, he made for the tool-house.

Lady saw whither he was bound. She ceased to follow. Wheeling about, she trotted stealthily back toward the stables. Reaching the tool-house door, the Master opened it and whistled to the unhappy young collie. Lady was nowhere in sight. At a second summons, she appeared from around the corner of the stables; moving close to the ground, and with many wriggles of protest. Twice, she stopped; and looked appealingly at the man.

The Master hardened his soul against the prettily pathetic appeal in her eyes and actions; and called her to him again. His own momentary anger against the luckless youngster was gone,—the more so since the eagle had not been damaged by its fall,—but he knew it was needful to impress strongly on Lady the fact of her punishment. This for her own sake as much as for his; since a housedog is worthless until it learns that each and every indoor object must be respected and held sacred from mutilation.

Wherefore, he was minded to spare Lady from any future punishment by making this present lesson sink deep into her brain. Disregarding her manifest aversion for the tool-house, he motioned her into it and shut the door behind her.

"You'll stay there, till morning," he told her, as he closed the window and glanced in at the forlorn little wisp of fur and misery. "You'll be comfortable. And the open spaces under the roof will give you all the air you want. I don't dare leave this window open, for fear you might be able to jump out. You've had your supper. And there's a pan of fresh water in there. You'll be no worse off there than you were all winter. A night in jail may teach you to be a decent, house-broke dog; and not a mutt."

As he was on the way back to his study, in the sunset, the car came down the drive, bearing the Mistress. Lad was seated in solemn joy on the front seat, at her side. The big collie loved motoring. And, as a rule, he was relegated to the back seat. But when the Mistress went out alone, his was the tremendously-enjoyed privilege of sitting in front, beside her.

"I had to lick Lady," reported the Master, shamefacedly, as he helped his wife from the car. "She went for the eagle in my study. You remember how I scolded her for that, last week, don't you? Well, that's all the good it did. And I had to whip her. I hated to. I'm glad you weren't here to look unhappy about it. Then I shut her up for the night in the tool-house. She—"

He broke off, to look at Lad.

As the collie had jumped down from the car and had started toward the house, he had struck Lady's trail; and he had followed it. It had led him to the tool-house. Finding Lady was locked inside and unhappy, he had come galloping back to the Master.

Standing in front of the man, and whining softly, he was scanning the faces of his two deities with troubled eagerness. Evidently, he considered that Lady had been locked in by mistake; and he was pleading for her release. As these humans did not seem to catch the idea his eyes and expression conveyed, he trotted a few steps toward the tool-house and then paused to look invitingly back at them.

Twice he did this. Then, coming up to the Master, he caught the latter's coat-hem lightly between his teeth and tugged on it as he backed toward the tool-house.

"No, old friend," said the Master, petting the silken head so appealingly upraised to him. "I know what you're getting at. But I can't let her out. Tomorrow morning. Not till then. Come on up to dinner."

Unwillingly and with wistful backward looks, Lad followed the Mistress and the Master to the house and into the dining room and to his wonted place on the floor at the Master's left side. But, more than once during the meal, the man caught the collie's eyes fixed on him in worried supplication; and was hard put to it not to grant the plea which fairly clamored in his chum's mute gaze.

After dinner, when the Mistress and the Master set off on their usual evening walk, Lad was not on hand to accompany them. As a rule, he was all around them and in front and behind, in a series of gay rushes, as they started on these walks. But not until the Master called him, tonight, did he appear. And then he came up dolorously from the tool-house.

Lad did not understand, at all, what was wrong. He knew only that Lady had been shut up in a place she detested and that she was horribly unhappy and that the Master would not let her out. It perplexed him; and it made him increasingly wretched. Not only did he miss his playfully capricious young mate, but her unhappiness made him heartsick.

Vainly, he tried to plead with the Master for her release, as the walk began; and again at its end.

There were such a lot of things in the world that even the

cleverest collie could not make head or tail of! And most of these things were sad.

That night, when the house was shut, Lad crept as usual into his cave under the piano. And he lay down with a sigh, his great head between his two absurdly small white forepaws. As a rule, before going to sleep for the night, Lad used to spend much time in licking those same snowy forepaws into shining cleanliness. The paws were his one gross vanity; and he wasted more than an hour a day in keeping them spotlessly white. But tonight he was too depressed to think of anything but the whimpering little dog imprisoned down in the tool-house.

After a while, he fell asleep.

A true watchdog sleeps with all his senses or the very edge of wakefulness. And when he wakens, he does not waken as do we humans;—yawningly, dazedly, drunk with slumber. At one moment he is sound asleep. At the next he is broad awake; with every faculty alert.

So ever it was, with Lad. So it was with him, this night. An hour before dawn, he woke with sharp suddenness; and at once he was on his feet; tense, on guard. He did not know what had roused him. Yet, now that he was awake, two of his senses recorded something which banished from him all thought of further sleep.

To his ears came a far-off muffled wail;—a wail which held more than unhappiness;—a wail which vibrated with real terror. And he knew the voice for Lady's.

To his sensitive nostrils, through the intervening distance and the obstructing walls and windows, drifted a faint reek of smoke.

Now, the smoke-smell, by itself, meant nothing whatever to Lad. All evening a trace of it had hung in the air; from the brush fire. And, in any case, this whiff was too slight to have emanated from the house or from any spot near the house. Yet, taken together with Lady's cry of fear—

Lad crossed to the front door, and scratched imperiously at it. The locked door did not yield to his push. Too sensible to keep on at a portal he could not open, he ran upstairs, to the closed door of the Master's room. There, again he scratched; this time harder and more loudly. Twice and thrice he scratched; whining under his breath.

At last the deep-slumbering Master heard him. Rousing himself, and still three-quarters asleep, he heard not only the scratching and the whimper but, in the distance, Lady's wail of fear. And, sleep-drugged, he mumbled:

"Shut up, Laddie!—I hear her.—Let her howl.—If she's lonely, down there, she'll—she'll remember the lesson—all the better. Go downstairs and—be quiet!"

He fell sound asleep again. Obedient to the slumbrous mandate, Lad turned and pattered mournfully away. But, he was not content to return to his own nap, with that terror-cry of Lady's echoing in his ears. And he made a second attempt to get out.

At each side of the piano, in the music room, was a long French window. Often, by day, Lad used to pass in or out of these door-like windows. He knew that they, as well as the doors, were a recognized means of exit. Now, with eagerly scratching paw, he pushed at the nearest of them.

The house was but carelessly locked at night. For Lad's presence downstairs was a better burglar-preventive than the best bolts ever forged. Tired and drowsy, the Master, this night, had neglected to bar the French windows.

The window gave, at Lad's vehement scratch; and swung outward on its hinges. A second later, the big dog was running at top speed toward the tool-house.

Now, the ways of the most insignificant brushfire are beyond the exact wisdom of man. Especially in droughty weather. When they knocked off work for the day, the two laborers had gone back to the blaze beyond the tool-house and conscientiously had scattered and stamped on its last visible remnants. The Master, too, coming home from his evening walk, had glanced toward the back garden and had seen no telltale spark to hint at life in the trampled fire.

Nevertheless, a scrap of ember, hidden from the men's gaze beneath a handful of dead leaves had refused to perish with its comrade-sparks. And, in the course of five hours, an industrious little flicker had ignited other bits of brush and of dried leafage and last year's weed stumps. The wind was in the north. And it had guided the course of the crawling thread of red. The advancing line had thrown out tendrils of scarlet, as it went.

Most of these had died, in the plowed ground. One had not. It had crept on, half-extinguished at times and again snapping merrily, until it had reached the tool-house. The shed-like room stood on low joists, with a clear space ten inches high between its flimsy board floor and the ground. And, in this space, the leaves of the preceding autumn had drifted in windrows. The persevering spark did the rest.

Lady woke from a fitful doze, to find herself choking from smoke. The boards of the floor were too hot for endurance. Between their cracks thin wavery slices of smoke were pouring upward into the room. The leaves had begun to ignite the floor-boards and the lower part of the ramshackle building's thin walls.

While the pain and humiliation of her whipping had not been able to wring a sound from the young thoroughbred, yet fright of this sort was afar different thing. Howling with panic terror, she dashed about the small enclosure, clawing frantically at door and scantling. Once or twice she made half-hearted effort to spring up at the closed window. But, from lack of running-space as well as from lack of nerve to make the high leap, she failed.

Across the lawn and door-yard and around the end of the stables thundered Lad. With the speed of a charging bull he came on. Before he reached the burning shack, he knew more of his mate's plight and peril than any human could have known.

Around the small building he whirled, so close to it that the flames at its base seared his mighty coat and blistered and blackened his white paws.

Then, running back a yard or so, he flung his eighty-pound

weight crashingly at the fastened door. The door, as it chanced, was well-nigh the only solid portion of the shack. And it held firm, under an impact that bruised the flying dog and which knocked him breathless to the fire-streaked ground.

At sound of her mate's approach, Lady had ceased wailing. Lad could hear her terrified whimpers as she danced frantically about on the red-hot boards. And the knowledge of her torture drove him momentarily insane.

Staggering up from his fall, he flung his splendid head back and, with muzzle to the clouded skies, he tore to shreds the solemn silences of the spring night with a wolf-howl; hideous in its savage grief, deafeningly loud.

As though the awesome yell had cleared his brain, he sprang to his feet amid the stinging embers; steady, alert, calm; with no hint of despair or of surrender.

His smarting eyes fixed themselves on the single dusty window of the tool-house. Its sill was a full five feet above ground. Its four small panes were separated by a wide old-fashioned cross-piece of hardwood and putty. The putty, from age, was as solid as cement. The whole window was a bare sixteen by twenty inches.

Lad ran back, once more, a few feet; his gaze fixed appraisingly on the window and measuring his distance with the sureness of a sharpshooter.

The big collie had made up his mind. His plan was formed. And as he was all-wise, with the eerie wisdom of the highest type of collie, there can be scant doubt he knew just what that plan entailed.

It was suicide. But, oh, it was a glorious suicide! Compared to it the love-sacrifices of a host of Antonys and Abelards and Romeos are but petty things. Indeed, its nearest approach in real life was perhaps Moore's idiotically beautiful boast:

Through the fiery furnace your steps I'll pursue;
To find you and save you:—or perish there, too!

The great dog gathered himself for the insane hero-deed. His shaggy body whizzed across the scarlet pattern of embers; then shot into the air. Straight as a flung spear he flew; hurtling through the flame-fringed billows of smoke.

Against the shut window he crashed, with the speed of a catapult. Against it he crashed; and clean through it, into the hell of smoke and fire and strangulation inside the shack.

His head had smashed the strong cross-piece of wood and dried putty and had crumpled it like so much wet paper. His giant shoulders had ripped the window-frame clean of its screws. Into the burning room spun Lad, amid a hail of broken glass and splintered wood.

To the fire-eaten floor he was hurled, close to his cowering and whimpering mate. He reeled to his feet, and stood there, shoulder to shoulder with Lady. His work was done.

And, yet, it was not in Sunnybank Lad's nature to be such a fool as is the usual melodrama hero. True, he had come to share Lady's fate, if he could not rescue her. Yet, he would not submit tamely to death, until every resource had been tried.

He glanced at the door. Already he had found by harsh experience that his strength availed nothing in the battering down of those strong panels. And he peered up, through the swirling red smoke, toward the oblong of window, whereby he had made his tumultuous entrance to the death-trap.

Again, he must have known how hopeless of achievement was the feat he was about to try. But, as ever, mere obstacles were not permitted to stand in Lad's way.

Wheeling, he seized Lady by the nape of the neck. With a mighty heave, he swung her clear of the hot floor. Gathering all his fierce strength into one sublime effort, he sprang upward toward the window; his mate hanging from his iron jaws.

Yes, it was a ridiculous thing to attempt. No dog, with thrice Lad's muscular strength, could have accomplished the impossibility of springing out through that high, narrow window, carrying a weight of fifty pounds between his teeth.

Lad's leap did not carry him half the distance he had aimed for. Back to the floor he fell, Lady with him.

Maddened by pain and by choking and by stark terror, Lady had not the wit to realize what Lad was attempting. All she knew was that he had seized her roughly by the neck, and had leaped in air with her; and had then brought her bangingly down upon the torturing hot boards. And her panic was augmented by delirious rage.

At Lad's face she flew, snarling murderously. One slash of her curving eyetooth laid bare his cheek. Then she drove for his throat.

Lad stood stock still. His only move was to interpose his shaggy shoulder to her ravening jaws. And, deep into the fur and skin and flesh of his shoulder her furious teeth shore their way.

It would have been child's play for him to have shaken her off and to have leaped to safety, alone, through the sash-less window.

Yet he stood where he was; his sorrowful eyes looking tenderly down upon the maddened youngster who was tearing into him so ferociously.

And that was the picture the Master beheld; as he flung open the door and blinked gaspingly through the smoke for the dog he had locked in.

Brought out of bed, on the jump, by Lad's unearthly wolf howl, he had smelt the smoke and had run out to investigate. But, not until he unbarred the tool-house door did he guess that Lady was not the burning shack's only prisoner.

"It'll be another six months before your wonderful coat grows out again, Laddie dear," observed the Mistress, next day, as she renewed the smelly wet cloths on Lad's burned and glass-cut body. "Dr. Hopper says so. But he says the rest of you will be as well as ever, inside of a fortnight. And he says Lady will be well, before you will. But, honestly, you'll never look as beautiful, again, to me, as you do this very minute. He—he said you look like a scarecrow. But you don't. You look like a—like a—a-What gorgeously splendid thing *does* he look like, dear?" she appealed to her husband.

"He looks," replied the Master, after deep thought, "he looks like *Lad*. And that's about the highest praise I know how to give him;—or give to anyone."

CHAPTER V.

THE STOWAWAY

There were but three collies on the Place, in those days. Lad; his dainty gold-and-white mate, Lady; and their fluffy and fiery wisp of a son, little Wolf.

When Wolf was a spoiled and obstreperous puppy of three months or so, Lady was stricken with distemper and was taken to a veterinary hospital. There, for something more than three months she was nursed through the scourging malady and through the chorea and pneumonia which are so prone to follow in distemper's dread wake.

Science amuses itself by cutting up and otherwise torturing helpless dogs in the unholy name of vivisection. But Science has not yet troubled itself to discover one certain cure or preventive for the distemper which yearly robs thousands of homes of their loved canine pets and guards. Apparently it is pleasanter for scientists to watch a screaming dog writhe under the knife in a research laboratory than to trouble about finding a way to abolish distemper; and thus of ridding the dog world of its worst scourge.

This is a digression from our story. But perhaps it is worth your remembering,—you who care about dogs.

Altogether, Lady was away from the Place for fifteen weeks.

And, in her absence, the unhappy Lad took upon himself the task of turning little Wolf from a pest into something approaching a decent canine citizen. It was no sinecure, this educating of the hot-tempered and undisciplined youngster. But Lad brought to it an elephantine patience and an uncannily wise brain. And, by the time Lady was brought back, cured, the puppy had begun to show the results of his sire's stern teachings.

Indeed, Lady's absence was the best thing that could have befallen

Wolf. For, otherwise, his training must needs have devolved upon the Mistress and the Master. And no mere humans could have done the job with such grimly gentle thoroughness as did Lad. Few dogs, except pointers or setters or collies, will deign to educate their puppies to the duties of life and of field and of house. But Lad had done the work in a way that left little to be asked for.

When Lady came home, her flighty brain seemed to have forgotten the fact that young Wolf was her once-adored son. Of her earlier capricious devotion to him, no trace remained. She sniffed in stand-offish inquiry at him; as at a stranger. And the scatterbrain pup remembered her no better than she remembered him. There is a wide gulf in intelligence between a three-month puppy and one six months old.

Yet,—perhaps because they were both excitable and mischievous and loved romping,—and because each was a novelty to the other— mother and son quickly formed a new friendship. From the more sedate and discipline-enforcing Lad, the youngster turned eagerly to chum-ship with this flighty gold-white stranger. And Lady, for similar reason, seemed to find ten times as much congeniality and fun in romping with Wolf as in playing with the less galvanically agile Lad.

In brief, Lady and little Wolf became inseparable companions;— this to the semi-exclusion of Lad.

The great collie did not resent this exclusion; nor did he try to regain his fast-slipping hold on Wolf's affections. Yet, in fashion that was more pathetic than ludicrous, he sought to win back Lady's waning affection. A bit clumsily, he tried to romp and gambol with her, as did Wolf. He tried to interest her, as of yore, in following his lead in break-neck forest gallops after rabbits or in gloriously exhilarating swims in the fire-blue lake at the foot of the lawn. To the pityingly on-looking Mistress and Master, he seemed like some general or statesman seeking to unbend in the games and chatter of a party of high school boys and girls.

But it was no use.

True, in the cross-country runs or the swirling charges after rabbits, neither Lady nor Wolf could keep up with Lad's flying stride. And a long swim, which scarce breathed Lad, would exhaust either or both of them.

But, they were young; and he was middle-aged. And, as in human relationships, that one sentence told the whole tragic story.

As well expect a couple of flyaway children to give up a game of tag in order to listen to the solemn discourse of an elderly uncle; as to make the fun-loving Lady and Wolf widen their selfish comradeship to include in it the steadier and older and infinitely wiser Lad.

Perforce, Lad was thrown more and more on the society of the Mistress and the Master. And, in their friendship, he was happy;—until he would chance to see his mate and his little son playing in wild ecstasy with a stick or ball, and would frisk bulkily over to join them. In a bare second or two, the demeanor of both showed him just what a grossly unwelcome interloper he was.

Whereat, after a wistfully miserable glance from one to the other of the exclusive pair, Lad would trot slowly back to his human deities; and, with a queerly sobbing little sigh, he would curl up at the Mistress's feet.

"It's a shame, Laddie!" declared the Mistress, at one such time. "It's a *shame!* Why, you are worth a million of those crazy playdogs! You're a million times wiser and beautifuller and more lovable. Why do you bother with them? Master and I are ever so much better company for you; and we love to have you with us. Stay right here, and forget them."

Lad, perhaps, understood the actual meaning of one word in ten of the advice. But he understood and loved the Mistress's sweet voice and the caress of her cool little hand; and the sympathy in her tone. It all meant much to Laddie. Very much indeed. And he laid his mighty head against her knee; happy in the comfort of touch and voice.

Nevertheless, that wistful glint was ever lurking in his deep-set eyes, nowadays. And his gayly trumpeting bark rang out less often and less jubilantly than of old. He took to moping. And he spent more time than before in his beloved "cave," under the music-room piano.

Moping and solitude are no more beneficial to dogs than to humans. The Master racked his brain for some way of bringing the splendid collie back to his olden spirits.

Luck, or fate, took the matter out of his hands.

The Mistress and the Master were invited to spend a week with some friends whose house stood in an ultra-restricted residential park, high up in the Catskills. By leaving the Place at sunrise, they could reach the Park, by motor, in time for afternoon tea.

At dawn, the car was brought to the door. Its tonneau was piled with luggage; and all was ready for a start as soon as the unappetizingly early breakfast could be swallowed.

Wolf and Lady, after following the car from the garage to the door, wearied of the uninspiring wait; and set forth at a hand-gallop for the woods. There, at dawning, the dew would lie heavy. And wet ground ever holds scent better than does dry. It would be easy to pick up and follow rabbit trails, through the damp.

Lad made as though to follow them. He ran out of the house and half-way up the drive in pursuit of their flashing gold-and-white flight. Neither turned a head at sound of his following steps. Neither slackened pace to include him in the hunt.

Always abnormally sensitive, the big collie noted this aloofness. And he came to an irresolute halt. For a moment, he stared after the two vanishing runaways; his plumed tail swaying ever so little, in groundless expectation of an invitingly glance or yelp from Lady. Then, tail and crest adroop, he turned slowly back toward the house.

From puppyhood, an odd trait of Lad's had caused amusement at the Place. Whenever he was unhappy or considered himself ill-treated, it was his way to hunt for something wherewith he might comfort himself. For instance, as a pup, a scolding for some petty misdeed would send him in search of his cherished flannel doll or his squeaking ball. In later years, the car had taken the place of these babyhood comforters.

Lad cared more for motoring than for any other amusement. In moments of stress he sometimes ran to the garage and curled himself up in the tonneau; as though in hope someone might take pity on his unhappiness and give him a drive. And, usually, somebody did.

Now, turning back, rebuffed, from the forest gallop, he caught sight of the car. Not in the garage, either; but at the front door; where its presence could mean nothing except an immediate ride.

With one high spring, Lad had cleared the ground and was over the closed tonneau door and amid a ruck of luggage and rugs. The rear seat was filled by a steamer-trunk, strapped tightly in place there. And the bottom of the car was annoyingly crowded by bumpy bags and other gear.

Still, by the simple and ancestral process of turning himself around several times, Lad was able to clear enough space on the floor to permit of his lying down; albeit in a very compact bunch.

He settled himself into place on the floor with a satisfied jounce which loosened a car-rug draped over the trunk. Down slithered the rug; and fell athwart the dog's shaggy back and one of the bags. It was not heavy enough to annoy Lad or hurt his feelings. And its draped folds served as the top of a sort of cave for him. On the whole, Lad rather enjoyed the rug's descent. It made his narrow resting-place snugger and warmer on this chilly early morning. Patiently, Lad lay there; waiting for the car to start.

He did not have long to wait. In another minute or two, the Mistress and the Master came out from breakfast; and got into the front seat. Then the car was breasting the winding slope of the drive, in first speed; the faint jar of the engine sending undulations over the mahogany-and-white coat of the stowaway dog. And, in a minute more, they were out on the smooth highway, headed for the distant Catskills.

Now, Lad had not the remotest notion he was a stowaway. On the few times when it had not been convenient to take him on drives, the Master had always bidden him stay at home. And when, at such times, the dog chanced already to be its the car, he had been ordered back to earth. There, was no way for Lad to know, this morning, that neither of the car's other occupants had seen him as he lay curled up on the floor, three-quarters hidden under the fallen rug. The luggage had been arranged in the tonneau, before breakfast. And nobody had given a second glance at it since then.

The sun was rising over a new-made world, alive with summer glory and thrilling with bird-songs. The air, later in the day, would be warm. But, at sunrise, it was sharp and bracing. The mystic wonder and the hush of dawn were still brooding over the earth. The hard white road stretched out, like a winding river, between banks of dew-gleaming verdure. The mountain-tops were glowing with the touch of the sun. In the deeper valleys floated a shimmering dusk.

The car sped swiftly along the empty highway; slowing down only as it spun through half-awakened villages; or checked its pace to allow a sleepy boy to drive a straggling bunch of cows across the road to pasturage.

For an hour or more, Lad lay cuddled under the rug in contented laziness. Then the recumbent posture tired him; and he sat up. As a rule, one or the other of his deities was wont to turn around, at intervals, and speak to him or pet him. Today, neither of them paid him the slightest attention. Still, the ride was a joy. And the surrounding country was new and interesting. So Lad had a good time, in spite of human neglect. After another hour or so, he curled up again, among the bags, and fell to drowsing.

A six-hour run, over good roads, brought the car to Kingston, at the gateway to the Catskills. Here, at a hotel entrance, the machine came to a standstill. The Master got out, and turned to help the Mistress to alight. It was the place they had decided on for luncheon. Another three hours, at most, would carry them to their destination.

A negro boy, loafing aimlessly at the street corner, had begun to whistle industriously to himself as the car slowed down. And he had wakened into active motion. Apparently, he remembered all at once an important mission on the other side of the street. For he set off at a swinging pace.

His course took him so near the back of the car that he had to turn out, a step or so, to avoid collision with it. He accompanied this turning-out maneuver by another which was less ostentatious, but more purposeful. Timing his steps, so as to pass by the rear of the car just as the Master was busy helping his wife to descend, the youth thrust an arm over the side of the tonneau, with the speed of a striking snake. His hand closed on the handle of a traveling bag, among the heap of luggage. Never slackening his pace, the negro gave a fierce yank at his plunder, to hoist it over the closed door.

In that tourist-ridden city, bag-stealing offered much profit. In the rare chance of detection when he was at work, the boy had only to plead over-zeal in trying to earn an honest dime by helping lift the luggage to the sidewalk.

It was a pretty bit of theft; and it betokened long and careful practice. Thus,—from the thief's standpoint,—it was almost a pity the brilliant effort was wasted. For wasted it was.

This young negro prided himself on his powers of speed and of silence, in plying his trade. And, today, though he proceeded to excel in the first of these qualities, he disgraced himself most woefully as regarded the second.

For he jerked his hand out of the tonneau far faster than he had thrust it in. As he did so, he woke the echoes with the most blood-curdling screech his leathern lungs could compass.

As his dusky fingers had closed on the bag, something viselike and relentless had fastened upon those same expert fingers; breaking two of them, and rending the flesh of the lower hand.

Lad, in rising to his feet, after his pleasant nap, at the slowing of the car, had been aware of that predatory hand; as it groped for the bag. Now, from puppyhood, Lad had been taught to regard everything in the car as under his own careful guardianship. Hence, he lunged forward and sank his terrible white teeth deep into the groping fingers.

By main force the youth tore free. With a second screech, he reeled back from the unseen peril which had assailed him. But Lad would not have it so.

There was a harsh-breathed growl, from down in the tonneau; and, on the instant, a tawny giant shape came catapulting over the top of the shut door and hurled itself upon the staggering negro.

The Master, turning at sound of the yell, was just in time to see the attack. The collie,—supposedly ninety miles away, and peacefully guarding the Place,—was hurtling through the air and crashing against the chest of a gray-faced and pop-eyed young negro. To earth went the two; in a cloud of dust; a second before the Master's sharp call brought Lad reluctantly away from his prey, and just as a policeman and a score of idlers came running up.

The thief did not wait to explain. No sooner did he see the Master catch the infuriated dog by the ruff than he scrambled to his feet; ducked under the policeman's arm and set off, around a corner, in something better than record time. Somehow, the encounter had deprived him of the nerve and the pluck to stand his ground and to explain that he had merely been trying to help with the luggage. His only desire, just then, was to put as many thousand miles as possible between himself and the tawny demon that had assaulted him.

"Laddie!" gasped the Mistress, unbelieving, as the policeman and most of the little crowd set off after the fugitive. "*Laddie!* What in the world—?"

"He—he must have been in the car, all the time," gabbled the Master, brilliantly. "He must have jumped in, while we were at breakfast. See, he's cleared a space for himself between two of the bags. He's been there, all the time, and we never—"

"If he hadn't been there," suggested the Mistress, "we'd be looking now for one or two pieces of luggage that had disappeared. When the Grays went through here, one of their suitcases was—"

"But what in blazes are we going to do with him?" broke in the Master, worriedly. "We can't take him all the way home. And I won't trust to sending him by express. He might get backed onto a siding and be kept there for days, without food or water. Besides, they won't let a dog go by express unless he's in a crate. What are we to do?"

"Why," said the Mistress, stooping to stroke the silken head that rested against her knee, "Why, Laddie seems to have settled that for us, by coming along. He's surely paid his way. We'll have to take him the rest of the trip. The Harmons will be glad to see him, I'm sure. Everybody's always glad to see Laddie, wherever we go. Let's take him. It's the only thing to do. We can explain to them how it happened."

And so, after more discussion, it was settled. Even as most things had a way of being settled when the Mistress proposed them.

Three hours later, the car stopped before the entrance of a roomily beautiful house in a roomily beautiful residence park, in the upper Catskills.

The welcoming smiles on the faces of host and hostess suffered sudden eclipse; as a huge mahogany-and-white collie stepped majestically from the car at the heels of the two guests.

"This is Lad," introduced the Mistress. "I hope you don't mind our bringing him. I can promise he won't be a bit of trouble to anybody. We didn't mean to bring him. It just happened. This was the way:—"

While she was recounting the adventure to Mrs. Harmon, their host drew the Master to one side.

"Say, old man," began Harmon, with visible discomfort, "please don't misunderstand me or anything. But I'm a little bothered about just what to do. This is the idea: There was a mad dog scare here in Daylight Park, last month, when a Pom puppy snapped at some kids that were teasing it. Then, a day or so later, a Persian cat had fits and chased old Mrs. Cratchitt across a lawn and gave her a spell of palpitation of the heart. And the next day an Angora goat that the Varian children had as a pet got loose and chewed up several hundred dollars' worth of lingerie off a line. Then the

Clives' spaniel took to barking under Rutherford Garretse's study window. And—"

"You needn't be afraid of Lad's doing any of those fool things," bragged the Master. "He behaves as well as any human. Better than most of them. He—"

"That isn't the point," said his host, with growing uneasiness. "You see, Daylight Park is run as a club. Home government and all that sort of thing. Well, these livestock fracases raised such a row that the club's Board of Governors has passed an ordinance, forbidding the keeping of any pet animals in the whole park. Nothing bigger than a canary bird can be harbored here. It's a hard-and-fast rule. It seemed the only way to save our whole summer colony from disruption. You know a livestock squabble can cause more ructions in a small community than—"

"I see," mused the Master, staring glumly after Lad who was just vanishing into the house in the wake of the Mistress and the unhappy Mrs. Harmon. "I see. H'm!"

He pondered for an instant, while his host shifted from foot to foot and looked apologetic. Then the Master spoke again.

"The only way out, that I see," he hazarded, "is for me to drive back home with Lad; and leave him there and come on here, tomorrow. I can—"

"Nothing of the sort!" protested Harmon, "There's an easier way than that. Wittsville is only a mile or so from the Park gates. They've got a fine boarding kennel there. Several of the Park's dogs were exiled to it, when our ordinance went into effect. Jump into the car, and we'll take your collie there in ten minutes. He'll be well treated. And you and your wife can go to see him, every day you're here. Come along. I—I hate to seem inhospitable about this thing. But you see for yourself how it is. We—"

"Certainly," assented the Master. "I'll go in and get him and explain to my wife. Don't let it make you feel uncomfortable. We both understand."

Which accounts for the fact that Lad, within the next half hour, was preparing to spend his first night away from home and from the two people who were his gods. He was not at all happy. It had been an interesting day. But its conclusion did not please Laddie, in any manner.

And, when things did not please Lad, he had a very determined fashion of trying to avoid them;—unless perchance the Mistress or the Master had decreed otherwise.

The Master had brought him to this obnoxious strange place. But he had not bidden Lad stay there. And the collie merely waited his chance to get out. At ten o'clock, one of the kennelmen made the night rounds. He swung open the door of the little stall in which Lad had been locked for the night. At least, he swung the door halfway open. Lad swung it the rest of the way.

With a plunge, the collie charged out through the opening portal, ducked between the kennelman's legs, reached the open gate of the enclosure in two more springs; and vanished down the road into the darkness.

As soon as he felt the highway under his feet, Lad's nose drooped earthward; and he sniffed with all his might. Instantly, he caught the scent he was seeking;—a scent as familiar to him as that of his own piano cave; the scent of the Place's car-tires.

It had taken Harmon and the Master the best part of ten minutes to drive through the park and to the boarding kennels. It took Lad less than half that time to reach the veranda of the Harmon house. Circling the house and finding all doors shut, he lay down on the mat; and settled himself to sleep there in what comfort he might, until the Mistress and the Master should come down in the morning and find him.

But the Harmons were late risers. And the sun had been up for some hours before any of the household were astir.

If Lad had been the professionally Faithful Hound, of storybooks, he would doubtless have waited on the mat until someone should come to let him in. But, after lying there until broad daylight, he was moved to explore this new section of the world. The more so, since house after house within range of his short vision showed signs of life and activity.

Several people passed and repassed along the private roadway in front of the Harmons' door; and nearly all of these paused to peer at Lad, in what seemed to the collie a most flattering show of interest.

At last, the dog got to his feet, stretched himself fore-and-aft, in true collie fashion; and trotted down the paved walk to the road. There for a moment, he stood hesitant. As he stood, he was surveying the scene;—not only with his eyes, but with those far stronger sense organs, his ears and his nostrils. His ears told him nothing of interest. His nose told him much. Indeed, before he had fairly reached the road, these nostrils had telegraphed to his brain an odor that not only was highly interesting, but totally new to him. Lad's experience with scents was far-reaching. But this smell lay totally outside all his knowledge or memory.

It was a rank and queer smell;—not strong enough, out there in the open, to register in a human-brain; but almost stingingly acute to the highly sensitized dog. It was an alluring scent; the sort of odor that roused all his curiosity and seemed to call for prompt investigation.

Nose to ground, Lad set off to trace the smell to its source. Strong as it was, it grew stronger and fresher at every step. Even a mongrel puppy could have followed it. Oblivious to all else, Lad broke into a canter; nose still close to earth; pleasurably excited and keenly inquisitive.

He ran along the private road for perhaps a hundred yards. Then, he wheeled in at another paved walk and ran up a low flight of veranda steps. The front door of a house stood invitingly open to the cool air of the morning. In through the doorway went Lad; unheeding the gobbling call of a maid-servant who was sweeping the far end of the veranda.

Lad did not know he was committing trespass. To him an open door had always meant permission to enter. And the enticingly rank scent was tenfold stronger indoors than out. Across a hallway he trotted, still sniffing; and up a flight of stairs leading to the second story of the house.

At the stairhead, a room door stood wide. And into this room led the odor. Lad went in. He was in a large and sunlit room; but in the most disorderly room he had ever set eyes on. The room needed airing, too. For all its four windows were closed, except one which was open for perhaps six inches from the top.

Lad circled the room, twice; from door to windows, and thence to center table and around the walls; pausing at one window sill and again at the threshold; picking his way daintily over heaps of litter on the floor. Yes, the room was full of the scent. But, whence the scent emanated, Lad could not, for the life of him, tell. The room gave him no clew. And, after a few minutes of futile investigation, he turned to depart.

At the stairhead, he came upon the same servant he had seen sweeping the veranda. She cried: "Shoo!" at him and brandished her broom. Lad, in offended dignity, stalked past her and out of the house.

His quest having proven vain, he betook himself to the Harmons', arriving there as the Mistress and the Master emerged upon the veranda in company with their hosts. In wild delight, Lad scampered up to the Mistress; his whole stately body wriggling in eager welcome, his tiny white forepaws patting at her feet, his muzzle thrusting itself into her cupped hand.

"Why, Lad!" she cried. "Laddie! We were so worried about you. They just phoned from the kennels that you had gotten away. I might have known you'd find your way to us. We—"

She got no further. Up the walk, from the road, came running an apoplectically red and puffing man of late middle age;—a man whose face bore traces of lather; and who was swathed in a purple bathrobe. Flapping slippers ill-covered his sockless feet.

The Master recognized the fast-advancing newcomer. He recognized him from many pictures in newspapers and magazines.

This was Rutherford Garretse, world-famed author and collector; the literary lion and chief celebrity of the summer colony at Daylight Park. But what eccentricity of genius could account for his costume and for this bellicose method of bearing down upon a neighbor's home, was more than the Master could guess.

Nor did the visitor's first words clear up the mystery. Halting at the foot of the steps, Rutherford Garretse gesticulated in dumb anguish, while he fought for breath and for coherent speech. Then, disregarding Harmon's wondering greeting, the celebrity burst into choking staccato speech.

"That dog!" he croaked. "That—that—DOG! The maid saw him go into the house. Saw him go up to my study. She was afraid to follow, at first. But in a few minutes she did. She saw him coming out of my study! COME!!! I demand it. All of you. *COME!*"

Without another word, he wheeled and made off down the road, pausing only to beckon imperiously. Marveling, the group on the veranda followed. Deaf to their questions, he led the way. Lad fell into line behind the perplexed Mistress.

Down the road to the next house, stalked Rutherford Garretse. At the doorway, he repeated his dramatic gesture and commanded: "*COME!*"

Up the broad stairs he stamped. Behind him trailed the dumfounded procession; Laddie still pattering happily along with the Mistress. At the open door of a large room at the stairhead, the author stood aside and pointed in silent despair through the doorway.

"What's up?" queried Harmon, for perhaps the tenth time. "Is anything—?"

His question ended in a grunt. And, like the others, he stared aghast on the scene before him.

The room, very evidently, was a study. But much of its floor, just now, was heaped, ankle high, with hundreds of pages of torn and crumpled paper.

The desk-top and a Sheraton cabinet and table were bare of

all contents. On the floor reposed countless shattered articles of glass and porcelain; jumbled together with blotters an pastepot and shears and ink-stand and other utensils. Ink had been poured in grotesque pattern on rugs and parquetry and window curtains.

In one corner lay a typewriter, its keys twisted and its carriage broken. Books—some of them in rare bindings,—lay gutted and ink-smeared, from one end of the place to the other.

Through the daze of general horror boomed the tremblingly majestic voice of Rutherford Garretse.

"I wanted you to see!" he declaimed. "I ordered everything left as it was. That mess of papers all over the floor is what remains of the first draft of my book. The book I have been at work on for six months! I—"

"And it was the dog, there!" sputtered the maid-servant; emotion riding over discipline. "I c'n swear the room was neat and all dusted. Not a blessed thing out of place; and all the paper where Mr. Garretse had stacked 'em in his portfolio, yonder. I dusted this study and then the dining room. And then I went out to sweep the veranda; like I always do, before breakfast. And maybe ten minutes later I see this brute trot out of Mr. Harmon's place, and along the road, and come, asnuffing up the steps and into the house. And when I followed him upstairs and scatted him out, I saw the room looking like it is, now; and I yells to Mr. Garretse, and he's shaving, and—"

"That will do, Esther!" snapped the author. "And, now, sir—"

"But, Mr. Garretse," put in the Mistress, "Lad never did such a thing as this, in all his life! He's been brought up in the house. Even as a puppy, he was—"

"The evidence shows otherwise," interrupted Garretse, with a visible struggle at self-control. "No human, unless he were a maniac, would have done such a wantonly destructive thing. No other animal has been here. The dog was seen entering and leaving this room. And my work of six months is not only destroyed by him, but many of the very best pieces in my glass-and-porcelain cabinet."

"But—"

"I consented to stay on at Daylight Park, only on the solemn assurance of the Governors that no animal should be allowed again within the Park precincts. I detest animals. Particularly dogs. And now I see my dislike is not mere prejudice. May I ask what the owners and—and the harborer—of the cur mean to do about this outrage? Notice, please, that I am speaking with studied moderation, in asking this vital question. I—"

"It is my fault,—or rather, it is a mistake,—that Lad is in the Park," spoke up the Master. "Mr. Harmon is wholly innocent in the matter. I can testify to that. If there is any fine or other penalty in connection with my dog's being here, I'm ready to settle for it. But if you expect me to believe that Laddie did all this weird damage to your manuscript and your collection and your room,—why, that's absurd! Utterly absurd! Lad, never in his life,—"

"The courts will think otherwise!" blazed Garretse, losing a fraction of his hard-held selfmastery. "And the case shall go through every court in the land, since you persist in this idiotic denial of a proven fact. I warn you, I shall—Look there!" he broke off, furiously, leveling a shakily vehement forefinger at Lad. "Watch him! He's prowling around, even now, in search of more things to injure. He—"

The author finished his sentence by catching up a heavy metal paperweight and drawing it back as if for a throw. His muscles flexed. The Mistress moved, as by accident, between the raging man and the dog.

The Master, for the moment, lacked presence of mind to do even that much for his canine chum's safety. He was too much taken up in glaring unbelievingly at Lad.

The sedate collie, after following the bevy of excited humans upstairs, had stood gravely, just inside the threshold; looking with keen interest from one to the other of the gesticulating and noisy group. Then, as a sharp whiff of that same baffling scent assailed his nose, he began a new tour of the room.

The odor was fresher than before. And Lad's curiosity was roused to the full. He sniffed to right and left, exploring the floor rubbish with inquiring muzzle, and circling the despoiled writing desk.

It was then that Garretse called attention to him. And it was then that Lad's nose suddenly pointed skyward. In another moment, he had bounded eagerly toward one of the windows,—the window that was slightly open from the top.

From that direction, the scent now came; and it was more potent than at any earlier time in his quest.

Even as the astonished eyes of the group followed Lad windowward, those same eyes were attracted by a partial darkening of the open space at the window's top.

Into the room, through the narrow aperture wiggled a hairy form, moving with eel-like speed.

Thence, it leaped to the floor. For the fraction of a second, the intruder crouched there; peering about, to determine into what company his jump had landed him.

He was a gray monkey, small, infinitely aged and withered of aspect. His paws and forearms were black with half-dry ink. Here and there, all over his fuzzy gray body, ink-blobs were spattered. In one skinny paw he still clutched the splintered fragment of a Satsuma vase.

By the time the gaping humans could get a single good look at the monkey, Lad was at him. Here at last was the solution of that mysterious scent, so new to the collie.

Lad galloped toward the wizened and malodorous gray bunch; more intent on investigation than on attack. The monkey did not wait for him. With an incredibly agile leap, he was on the spattered window curtains and swarming up to the rod at the top. There he squatted, well out of reach; grimacing horribly and chattering in simian wrath.

"It's—it's a devil!" stammered Rutherford Garretse; his nearsighted eyes squinting as he sought to take in the motley details of the creature's appearance. "I—"

"It's Mrs. McMurdle's pest of a monkey, sirs" blithered the

maid. "Asking your pardon. The one she made such a fuss about sending away, last month, when all beastees was barred from the Park. It must 'a' strayed back from where she sent it to, the crafty little nuisance! It's—"

"Incidentally," said the Master, "it is the creature that wrecked your room. See the ink on it. And that bit of porcelain it's brandishing at us looks like a match for some of these smashed bits on the floor. It got in here, I suppose, through that window, earlier,—and—"

"No," corrected the Mistress, wiser at deduction. "Through the doorway, downstairs. From somewhere outside. Probably while the maid was dusting the dining-room. It came in here and began destroying things; as monkeys love to. And Laddie struck its trail and followed it up here. It heard Lad coming and it got out through the window. Then, just now, something outside scared it; and it climbed back in again. I wonder if—"

As she talked, the Mistress had moved toward the nearest window.

"See?" she finished, in triumph, as she pointed out and down.

On the patch of back lawn, below, stood a very much flustered old lady, her worried gaze upraised to the study. In one hand she carried a leash, in the other a half-peeled banana.

"It's Mrs. McMurdle!" exclaimed Harmon. "The maid was right. She must have disobeyed the ordinance and had the miserable monkey hidden in her house all the time. It must have gotten out, this morning; and she hunted around till she saw it perched on the top of the window cornice. I suppose it dived back in here, at sight of her. She—"

"Come on, Laddie!" whispered the Mistress, under cover of a new outbreak of multiple talk. "*You're* acquitted, anyhow. And the rest of the scene is really no business of ours. The sooner we get you to the boarding kennels again, the less chance there is of trouble. And Master and I will come to see you there, every single day, till we go back home."

A week later, the car turned in again at the gates of the Place. This time, Lad rode in state atop the flat trunk on the rear seat. As the car halted at the veranda, he sprang to earth without waiting for the tonneau door to be opened.

For, dashing toward him from the direction of the lake, Lady hove in sight. Behind her, and trotting more leisurely, came Wolf. At sight and scent of her returned mate, Lady fairly squealed with delight. She whirled up to Lad, frantically licking his face and spinning about him with little staccato yelps of joy.

Lad was deliriously happy. Not only was he at home again; but Lady was welcoming him with an effusion that she had not shown him for many a sorrowful month. He could not understand it. Nor did he try to. He was content to accept the miracle; and to rejoice in it with all his great honest heart.

Knowing nothing of feminine psychology, he could not realize that a week of Puppy Wolf's sole and undiluted companionship had bored Lady horribly and had begun to get on her nerves;—nor that she had learned to miss and yearn for the big, wise, ever-gentle mate whom she had so long neglected.

It was enough for Lad to know that he was no longer a neglected outsider, in the Place's canine family; but that his worshiped mate was wild with joy to see him again.

"Look!" said the Master. "The old chap has forgiven her for every bit of her rottenness to him. He's insanely happy, just because she chooses to make much of him, once more."

"Yes," assented the Mistress, cryptically "Sometimes dogs are pitifully—human!"

CHAPTER VI.
THE TRACKER

The child's parents were going to Europe for three months, that winter. The child himself was getting over a nervous ailment. The doctors had advised he be kept out of school for a term; and be sent to the country.

His mother was afraid the constant travel from place to place, in Europe, might be too much for him. So she asked leave of the Mistress and the Master,—one of whom was her distant relative,—for the convalescent to stay at the Place during his parents' absence.

That was how it all started.

The youngster was eleven years old; lank and gangling, and blest with a fretful voice and with far less discipline and manners than a three-month collie pup. His name was Cyril. Briefly, he was a pest,—an unspeakable pest.

For the first day or two at the Place, the newness of his surroundings kept Cyril more or less in bounds. Then, as homesickness and novelty alike wore off, his adventurous soul expanded.

He was very much at home; far more so than were his hosts, and infinitely more pleased than they with the situation in general. He had an infinite genius for getting into trouble. Not in the delightfully normal fashion of the average growing boy; but in furtively crafty ways that did not belong to healthy childhood.

Day by day, Cyril impressed his odd personality more and more on everything around him. The atmosphere of sweet peace which had brooded, like a blessing, over the whole Place, was dispersed.

The cook,—a marvel of culinary skill and of long service, gave tearful warning, and departed. This when she found the insides of all her cooking utensils neatly soaped; and the sheaf of home-letters in her work-box replaced by cigar-coupons.

One of the workmen threw over his job with noisy blasphemy; when his room above the stables was invaded by stealth and a comic-paper picture of a goat's head substituted for his dead mother's photograph in the well-polished little bronze frame on his bureau.

And so on, all along the line.

The worst and most continuous sufferer from Cyril's loathed presence on the Place was the massive collie, Lad.

The child learned, on the first day of his visit, that it would be well-nigh as safe to play with a handful of dynamite as with Lad's gold-and-white mate, Lady. Lady did not care for liberties from anyone. And she took no pains to mask her snappish first-sight aversion to the lanky Cyril. Her fiery little son, Wolf, was scarce less formidable than she, when it came to being teased by an outsider. But gallant old Lad was safe game.

He was safe game for Cyril, because Lad's mighty heart and soul were miles above the possibility of resenting anything from so pitifully weak and defenseless a creature as this child. He seemed to realize, at a glance, that Cyril was an invalid and helpless and at a physical disadvantage. And, as ever toward the feeble, his big nature went out in friendly protection to this gangling wisp of impishness.

Which was all the good it did him.

In fact, it laid the huge collie open to an endless succession of torment. For the dog's size and patience seemed to awaken every atom of bullying cruelty in the small visitor's nature.

Cyril, from the hour of his arrival, found acute bliss in making Lad's life a horror. His initial step was to respond effusively to the collie's welcoming advances; so long as the Mistress and the Master chanced to be in the room. As they passed out, the Mistress chanced to look back.

She saw Cyril pull a bit of cake from his pocket and, with his left hand, proffer it to Lad. The tawny dog stepped courteously forward to accept the gift. As his teeth were about to close daintily on the cake, Cyril whipped it back out of reach; and with his other hand rapped Lad smartly across the nose.

Had any grown man ventured a humiliating and painful trick of that sort on Lad, the collie would have been at the tormentor's throat, on the instant. But it was not in the great dog's nature to attack a child. Shrinking back, in amaze, his abnormally sensitive feelings jarred, the collie retreated majestically to his beloved "cave" under the music-room piano.

To the Mistress's remonstrance, Cyril denied most earnestly that he had done the thing. Nor was his vehemently tearful denial shaken by her assertion that she had seen it all.

Lad soon forgave the affront. And he forgave a dozen other and worse mal-treatments which followed. But, at last, the dog took to shunning the neighborhood of the pest. That availed him nothing; except to make Cyril seek him out in whatsoever refuge the dog had chosen.

Lad, trotting hungrily to his dinner dish, would find his food thick-strewn with cayenne pepper or else soaked in reeking gasoline.

Lad, seeking peace and solitude in his piano cave, would discover his rug, there, cleverly scattered with carpet tacks, points upward.

Lad, starting up from a snooze at the Mistress's call, would be deftly tripped as he started to bound down the veranda steps, and would risk bruises and fractures by an ugly fall to the driveway below.

Wherever Lad went, whatever Lad did, there was a cruel trick awaiting him. And, in time, the dog's dark eyes took on an expression of puzzled unhappiness that went straight to the hearts of the two humans who loved him.

All his life, Lad had been a privileged character on the Place. Never had he known nor needed whip or chain. Never had he,—or any of the Place's other dogs,—been wantonly teased by any human. He had known, and had given, only love and square treatment and stanch friendliness. He had ruled as benevolent monarch of the Place's Little People; had given loyal service to his two deities, the Mistress and the Master; and had stood courteously aloof from the rest of mankind. And he had been very, very happy.

Now, in a breath, all this was changed. Ever at his heels, ever waiting to find some new way to pester him, was a human too small and too weak to attack;—a human who was forever setting the collie's high-strung nerves on edge or else actively hurting him. Lad could not understand it. And as the child gained in health and strength, Lad's lot grew increasingly miserable.

The Mistress and the Master were keenly aware of conditions. And they did their best,—a useless best,—to mitigate them for the dog. They labored over Cyril, to make him leave Lad alone. They pointed out to him the mean cowardice of his course of torture. They even threatened to send him to nearer relatives until his parents' return. All in vain. Faced with the most undeniable proofs, the child invariably would lie. He denied that he had ever ill-used Lad in any way; and would weep, in righteous indignation, at the charges. What was to be done?

"I thought it would brighten up the house so, to have a child in it again!" sighed the Mistress as she and her husband discussed the matter, uselessly, for the fiftieth time, after one of these scenes. "I looked forward so much to his coming here! But he's—oh, he isn't like any child I ever heard of before!"

"If I could devote five busy minutes a day to him," grunted the Master, "with an axe-handle or perhaps a bale-stick—"

"You wouldn't do it!" denied his wife. "You wouldn't harm him; any more than Lad does. That's the trouble. If Cyril belonged to us, we could punish him. Not with a—a balestick, of course. But he needs a good wholesome spanking, more than anyone else I can think of. That or some other kind of punishment that would make an impression on him. But what can we do? He isn't ours—"

"Thank God!" interpolated the Master, piously.

"And we can't punish other people's child," she finished. "I don't know what we *can* do. I wouldn't mind half so much about the other sneaky things he does; if it wasn't for the way he treats Laddie. I—"

"Suppose we send Lad to the boarding kennels, at Ridgewood, till the brat is gone?" suggested the Master. "I hate to do it. And the good old chap will be blue with homesickness there. But at least he'll get kind treatment. When he comes over to me and looks up into my eyes in that terribly appealing way, after Cyril has done some rotten thing to him,—well, I feel like a cur, not to be able to justify his faith that I can make things all right for him. Yes, I think I'll send him to the boarding kennels. And, if it weren't for leaving you alone to face things here, I'd be tempted to hire a stall at the kennels for myself, till the pest is gone."

The next day, came a ray of light in the bothered gloom. And the question of the boarding kennels was dropped. The Mistress received a letter from Cyril's mother. The European trip had been cut short, for business reasons; and the two travelers expected to land in New York on the following Friday.

"Who dares say Friday is an unlucky day?" chortled the Master in glee, as his wife reached this stage of the letter.

"And," the Mistress read on, "we will come out to the Place, on the noon train; and take darling Cyril away with us. I wish we could stay longer with you; but Henry must be in Chicago on Saturday night. So we must catch a late afternoon train back to town, and take the night train West. Now, I—"

"Most letters are a bore," interpolated the Master. "Or else they're a bother. But this one is a pure rapture. Read it more slowly, won't, you, dear? I want to wallow in every blessed word of hope it contains. Go ahead. I'm sorry I interrupted. Read on. You'll never have such another enthusiastic audience."

"And now," the Mistress continued her reading, "I am going to ask both of you not to say a single word to precious Cyril about our coming home so soon. We want to surprise him. Oh, to think what his lovely face will be like, when he sees us walking in!"

"And to think what *my* lovely face will be like, when I see him walking out!" exulted the Master. "Laddie, come over here. We've got the gorgeousest news ever! Come over and be glad!"

Lad, at the summons, came trotting out of his cave, and across the room. Like every good dog who has been much talked to, he was as adept as any dead-beat in reading the varying shades of the human voice. The voices and faces alike of his two adored deities told him something wonderful had happened. And, as ever, he rejoiced in their gladness. Lifting his magnificent head, he broke into a salvo of trumpeting barks; the oddly triumphant form of racket he reserved for great moments.

"What's Laddie doing?" asked Cyril, from the threshold. "He sounds as if he was going mad or something."

"He's happy," answered the Mistress.

"Why's he happy?" queried the child.

"Because his Master and I are happy," patiently returned the Mistress.

"Why are *you* happy?" insisted Cyril.

"Because today is Thursday," put in the Master. "And that means tomorrow will be Friday."

"And on Friday," added the Mistress, "there's going to be a beautiful surprise for you, Cyril. We can't tell you what it is, but—"

"Why can't you tell me?" urged the child. "Aw, go ahead and tell me! I think you might."

The Master had gone over to the nearest window; and was staring out into the gray-black dusk. Mid-winter gripped the dead world; and the twilight air was deathly chill. The tall naked treetops stood gaunt and wraithlike against a leaden sky.

To the north, the darkness was deepest. Evil little puffs of gale stirred the powdery snow into myriads of tiny dancing white devils. It had been a fearful winter, thus far; colder than for a score of years; so cold that many a wild woodland creature, which usually kept far back in the mountains, had ventured down nearer to civilization for forage and warmth.

Deer tracks a-plenty had been seen, close up to the gates of the Place. And, two days ago, in the forest, half a mile away, the Master had come upon the half-human footprints of a young bear. Starvation stalked abroad, yonder in the white hills. And need for provender had begun to wax stronger among the folk of the wilderness than their inborn dread of humans.

"There's a big snowstorm coming up," ruminated the Master, as he scanned the grim weather-signs. "A blizzard, perhaps. I—I hope it won't delay any incoming steamers. I hope at least one of them will dock on schedule. It—"

He turned back from his musings, aware for the first time that a right sprightly dialogue was going on. Cyril was demanding for the eighth time:

"*Why* won't you tell me? Aw, I think you might! What's going to happen that's so nice, Friday?"

"Wait till Friday and see," laughed the Mistress.

"Shucks!" he snorted. "You might tell me, now. I don't want to wait and get s'prised. I want to know, *now*. Tell me!"

Under her tolerant smile, the youngster's voice scaled to an impatient whine. He was beginning to grow red.

"Let it go at that!" ordained the Master. "Don't spoil your own fun, by trying to find out, beforehand. Be a good sportsman."

"Fun!" snarled Cyril. "What's the fun of secrets? I want to know—"

"It's snowing," observed the Mistress, as a handful of flakes began to drift past the windows, tossed along on a puff of wind.

"I want to *know*!" half-wept the child; angry at the change of subject, and noting that the Mistress was moving toward the next room, with Lad at her heels. "Come back and tell me!"

He stamped after her to bar her way. Lad was between the irate Cyril and the Mistress. In babyish rage at the dog's placid presence in his path, he drew back one ungainly foot and kicked the astonished collie in the ribs.

At the outrage, Lad spun about, a growl in his throat. But he forbore to bite or even to show his teeth. The growl had been of indignant protest at such unheard-of treatment; not a menace. Then the dog stalked haughtily to his cave, and lay down there.

But the human witnesses to the scene were less forbearing;—being only humans. The Mistress cried out, in sharp protest at the little brute's action. And the Master leaned forward, swinging Cyril clear of the ground. Holding the child firmly, but with no roughness, the Master steadied his own voice as best he could; and said:—

"This time you've not even bothered to wait till our backs were turned. So don't waste breath by crying and saying you didn't do it. You're not my child; so I have no right to punish you. And I'm not going to. But I want you to know you've just kicked something that's worth fifty of you."

"You let me down!" Cyril snarled.

"Lad is too white and clean and square to hurt anything that can't hit back," continued the Master. "And you are not. That's the difference between you. One of the several million differences,—all of them in Lad's favor. When a child begins life by being cruel to dumb animals, it's a pretty bad sign for the way he's due to treat his fellow-humans in later years,—if ever any of them are at his mercy. For your own sake, learn to behave at least as decently as a dog. If—"

"You let me down, you big bully!" squalled Cyril, bellowing with impotent fury. "You let me down! I—"

"Certainly," assented the Master, lowering him to the floor. "I didn't hurt you. I only held you so you couldn't run out of the room, before I'd finished speaking; as you did, the time I caught you putting red pepper on Lad's food. He—"

"You wouldn't dare touch me, if my folks were here, you big bully!" screeched the child, in a veritable mania of rage; jumping up and down and actually foaming at the mouth. "But I'll tell 'em on you! See if I don't! I'll tell 'em how you slung me around and said I was worsen a dirty dog like Lad. And Daddy'll lick you for it. See if he don't! He—"

The Master could not choke back a laugh; though the poor Mistress looked horribly distressed at the maniac outburst, and strove soothingly to check it. She, like the Master, remembered now that Cyril's doting mother had spoken of the child's occasional fits of red wrath. But this was the first glimpse either of them had had of these. Hitherto, craft had served Cyril's turn better than fury.

At sound of the Master's unintentional laugh the unfortunate child went quite beside himself in his transport of rage.

"I won't stay in your nasty old house!" he shrieked. "I'm going to the very first house I can find. And I'm going to tell 'em how you hammered a little feller that hasn't any folks here to stick up for him. And I'll get 'em to take me in and send a tel'gram to Daddy and Mother to come save me. I—"

To the astonishment of both his hearers, Cyril broke off chokingly in his yelled tirade; caught up a bibelot from the table, hurled it with all his puny force at Lad, the innocent cause of the fracas; and then rushed from the room and from the house.

The Mistress stared after him, dumfounded; his howls and the jarring slam of the house door echoing direfully in her ears. It was the Master who ended the instant's hush of amaze.

"Whenever I've heard a grown man say he wished he was a boy again," he mused, "I always set him down for a liar. But, for once in my life, I honestly wish I was a boy, once more. A boy one day younger and one inch shorter and one pound lighter than Cyril. I'd follow him out of doors, yonder, and give him the thrashing of his sweet young life. I'd—"

"Oh, do call him back!" begged the Mistress. "He'll catch his death of cold, and—"

"Why will he?" challenged the Master, without stirring. "For all his noble rage, I noticed he took thought to grab up his cap and his overcoat from the hall, as he wafted himself away. And he still had his arctics on, from this afternoon. He won't—"

"But suppose he should really go over to one of the neighbors," urged the Mistress, "and tell such an awful story as he threatened to? Or suppose—"

"Not a chance!" the Master reassured her. "Now that the summer people are away, there isn't an occupied house within half a mile of here. And he's not going to trudge a half-mile through the snow, in this bitter cold, for the joy of telling lies. No, he's down at the stables or else he's sneaked in through the kitchen; the way he did that other time when he made a grandstand exit after I'd ventured to lecture him on his general rottenness. Remember how worried about him you were, that time; till we found him sitting in the kitchen and pestering the maids? He—"

"But that time, he was only sulky," said the Mistress. "Not insanely angry, as he is now. I do hope—"

"Stop worrying!" adjured the Master. "He's all right."

Which proved, for perhaps the trillionth time in history, that a woman's intuitions are better worth following than a man's saner logic. For Cyril was not all right. And, at every passing minute he was less and less all right; until presently he was all wrong.

For the best part of an hour, in pursuance of her husband's counsel, the Mistress sat and waited for the prodigal's return. Then, surreptitiously, she made a round of the house; sent a man to ransack the stables, telephoned to the gate lodge, and finally came into the Master's study, big-eyed and pale.

"He isn't anywhere around," she reported, frightened. "It's dinner time. He's been gone in hour. Nobody's seen him. He isn't on the Place. Oh, I wonder if—"

"H'm!" grumbled her husband. "He's engineering an endurance contest, eh? Well, if he can stand it, we can."

But at sight of the deepening trouble in his wife's face, he got up from his desk. Going out into the hall, he summoned Lad.

"We might shout our heads off," he said, "and he'd never answer; if he's really trying to scare us. That's part of his lovable nature. There's just one way to track him, in double time. *Lad!*"

The Master had been drawing on his mackinaw and hipboots as he spoke. Now he opened the front door.

"Laddie!" he said, very slowly and incisively to the expectantly eager collie. "Cyril! Find *Cyril! Find* him!"

To the super-wise collie, there was nothing confusing in the command. Like many another good dog, he knew the humans of the household by their names; as well as did any fellow-human. And he knew from long experience the meaning of the word, "Find!"

Countless times that word had been used in games and in earnest. Its significance, now, was perfectly plain to him. The Master wanted him to hunt for the obnoxious child who so loved to annoy and hurt him.

Lad would rather have found anyone else, at the Master's behest. But it did not occur to the trained collie to disobey. With a visible diminishing of his first eager excitement, but with submissive haste, the big dog stepped out on to the veranda and began to cast about in the drifts at the porch edge.

Immediately, he struck Cyril's shuffling trail. And, immediately, he trotted off along the course.

The task was less simple than ordinarily. For, the snow was coming down in hard-driven sheets; blotting out scent almost as effectively as sight. But not for naught had a thousand generations of Lad's thoroughbred ancestors traced lost sheep through snowstorms on the Scottish moors. To their grand descendant they had transmitted their weird trailing power, to the full. And the scent of Cyril, though faint and fainter, and smothered under swirling snow, was not too dim for Lad's sensitive nostrils to catch and hold it.

The Master lumbered along, through the rising drifts, as fast as he could. But the way was rough and the night was as black dark as it was cold. In a few rods, the dog had far outdistanced him. And, knowing how hard must be the trail to follow by sense of smell, he forbore to call back the questing collie, lest Lad lose the clew altogether. He knew the dog was certain to bark the tidings when he should come up with the fugitive.

The Master by this time began to share his wife's worry. For the trail Lad was following led out of the grounds and across the highway, toward the forest.

The newborn snowstorm was developing into a very promising little blizzard. And the icy lash of the wind proved the fallacy of the old theory, "too cold to snow." Even by daylight it would have been no light task to steer a true course through the whirling and blinding storm. In the darkness, the man found himself stumbling along with drunkenly zigzag steps; his buffeted ears strained, through the noise of the wind for sound of Lad's bark.

But no such sound came to him. And, he realized that snow and adverse winds can sometimes muffle even the penetrating bark of a collie. The man grew frightened. Halting, he shouted with all the power of his lungs. No whimper from Cyril answered the hail. Nor, at his master's summons, did Lad come bounding back through the drifts. Again and again, the Master called.

For the first time in his obedient life, Lad did not respond to the call. And the Master knew his own voice could not carry, for a single furlong, against wind and snowfall.

"I'll go on for another half-hour," he told himself, as he sought to discern the dog's all-but obliterated footsteps through the deepening snow. "And then I'll go back and raise a search party."

He came to a bewildered stop. Fainter and more indistinguishable had Lad's floundering tracks become. Now,—by dint of distance and snow,—they ceased to be visible in the welter of drifted whiteness under the glare of the Master's flashlight.

"This means a search-party," decided the man.

And he turned homeward, to telephone for a posse of neighbors.

Lad, being only a dog, had no such way of sharing his burden. He had been told to find the child. And his simple code of life and of action left him no outlet from doing his duty; be that duty irksome or easy. So he kept on. Far ahead of the Master, his keen ears had not caught the sound of the shouts. The gale and the snow muffled them and drove them back into the shouter's throat. Cyril, naturally, had not had the remotest intent of laboring through the bitter cold and the snow to the house of any neighbor; there to tell his woeful tale of oppression. The semblance of martyrdom, without its bothersome actuality, was quite enough for his purpose. Once before, at home, when his father had administered a mild and much-needed spanking, Cyril had made a like threat; and had then gone to hide in a chum's home, for half a day; returning to find his parents in agonies of remorse and fear, and ready to load him with peace-offerings. The child saw no reason why the same tactics should not serve every bit as triumphantly, in the present case.

He knew the maids were in the kitchen and at least one man was in the stables. He did not want his whereabouts to be discovered before he should have been able to raise a healthy and dividend-bringing crop of remorse in the hearts of the Mistress and the Master, so he resolved to go farther afield.

In the back of the meadow, across the road, and on the hither side of the forest, was a disused cattle-barrack, with two stalls under its roof-pile of hay. The barrack was one of Cyril's favorite playhouses. It was dry and tight. Through his thick clothing he was not likely to be very cold, there, for an hour or two. He could snuggle down in the warm hay and play Indians, with considerable comfort; until such time as the fright and penitence of his hosts should have come to a climax and make his return an ovation.

Meanwhile, it would be fun to picture their uneasiness and fear for his safety; and to visualize their journeyings through the snow to the houses of various neighbors, in search of the lost child.

Buoyed up by such happy thoughts as these, Cyril struck out at a lively pace for the highroad and into the field beyond. The barrack, he knew, lay diagonally across the wide meadow, and near the adjoining woods. Five minutes of tramping through the snow ought to bring him to it. And he set off, diagonally.

But, before he had gone a hundred yards, he lost his first zest in the adventure. The darkness had thickened; and the vagrant wind-gusts had tightened into a steady gale; a gale which carried before it a blinding wrack of stingingly hard-driven snow.

The gray of the dying dusk was blotted out. The wind smote and battered the spindling child. Mechanically, he kept on for five or six minutes, making scant and irregular progress. Then, his spirit wavered. Splendid as it would be to scare these hateful people, there was nothing splendid in the weather that numbed him with cold and took away his breath and half-blinded him with snow.

What was the fun of making others suffer; if he himself were suffering tenfold more? And, on reaching the barrack, he would have all that freezing and blast-hammering trip back again. Aw, what was the use?

And Cyril came to a halt. He had definitely abandoned his high enterprise. Turning around, he began to retrace his stumbling steps. But, at best, in a large field, in a blizzard and in pitch darkness, and with no visible landmarks, it is not easy to double back on one's route, with any degree of accuracy. In Cyril's case, the thing was wholly impossible.

Blindly, he had been traveling in an erratic half-circle. Another minute of walking would have brought him to the highroad, not far from the Place's gateway. And, as he changed his course, to seek the road, he moved at an obtuse angle to his former line of march.

Thus, another period of exhausting progress brought him up with a bump against a solid barrier. His chilled face came into rough contact with the top rail of a line fence.

So relieved was the startled child by this encounter that he forgot to whine at the abrasion wrought upon his cheek by the rail. He had begun to feel the first gnawings of panic. Now, at once, he was calm again. For he knew where he was. This was the line fence between the Place's upper section and the land of the next neighbor.

All he need do was to walk along in the shelter of it, touching the rails now and then to make certain of not straying, until he should come out on the road, at the gate lodge. It was absurdly easy; compared to what he had been undergoing. Besides, the lee of the fence afforded a certain shelter from wind and snow. The child realized he had been turned about in the dark; and had been going in the wrong direction. But now, at last, his course seemed plain to him.

So he set off briskly, close to the fence;—and directly away from the nearby road.

For another half-hour he continued his inexplicably long tramp; always buoyed up by the hope of coming to the road in a few more steps; and doggedly sure of his bearings. Then, turning out from the fence, in order to skirt a wide hazel thicket, he tripped over an outcrop of rock, and tumbled into a drift. Getting to his feet, he sought to regain the fence; but the fall had shaken his senses and he floundered off in the opposite direction. After a rod or two of such futile plunging, a stumbling step took him clean off the edge of the world, and into the air.

All this, for the merest instant. Then, he landed with a jounce in a heap of brush and dead leaves. Squatting there, breathless, he stretched out his mittened hand, along the ground. At the end of less than another yard of this exploring, his fingers came again to the edge of the world and were thrust out over nothingness.

With hideous suddenness, Cyril understood where he was; and what had happened to him and why. He knew he had followed the fence for a full mile, *away* from the road; through the nearer woods, and gradually upward until he had come the line of hazels on the lip of the ninety-foot ravine which dipped down into a swamp-stretch known as "Pancake Hollow."

That was what he had done. In trying to skirt the hazels, he had stepped over the cliff-edge, and had dropped five feet or more to a rather narrow ledge that juts out over the ravine.

Well did he remember this ledge. More than once, on walks with the Mistress and the Master, he had paused to look down on it and to think fun it would be to imprison someone there and to stand above, guying the victim. It had been a sweet thought. And now, he, himself, was imprisoned there.

But for luck, he might have fallen the whole ninety feet; for the ledge did not extend far along the face of the cliff. At almost any other spot his tumble might have meant—

Cyril shuddered a little; and pursued the grisly theme no further. He was safe enough, till help should come. And, here, the blast of the wind did not reach him. Also, by cuddling low in the litter of leaves and fallen brush, he could ward off a little of the icy cold.

He crouched there; shaking and worn out. He was only eleven. His fragile body had undergone a fearful hour of toil and hardship.

As he was drawing in his breath for a cry to any chance searchers, the boy was aware of a swift pattering, above his head. He looked up. The sky was shade or two less densely black than the ravine edge. As Cyril gazed in terror, a shaggy dark shape outlined itself against the sky-line, just above him.

Having followed the eccentric footsteps of the wanderer, with great and greater difficulty, to the fence-lee where the tracing was much easier, Lad came to the lip of the ravine a bare five minutes after the child's drop to the ledge.

There, for an instant, the great dog stood; ears cocked, head inquiringly on one side; looking down upon the ledge. Cyril shrank to a quivering little heap of abject terror, at sight of the indistinct animal shape looming mountain-high above.

This for the briefest moment. Then back went Lad's head in a pealing bark that seemed to fill the world and to reecho from a myriad directions at once. Again and again, Lad gave clamorous voice to his discovery of the lost child.

On a clear or windless night, his racket must have penetrated to the dullest ears at the Place, and far beyond. For the bark of a dog has more carrying power than has any other sound of double its volume. But, in the face of a sixty-mile gale laden with tons of flying snow, the report of a cannon could scarce have carried over the stretch of windswept ground between the ravine and the Place.

Lad seemed to understand this. For, after a dozen thunderous barks, he fell silent; and stood again, head on one side, in thought.

At first sound of the barking, Cyril had recognized the dog. And his terror had vanished. In its place surged a peevish irritation against the beast that had so frightened him. He groped for a rock-fragment to hurl up at the rackety collie.

Then, the child paused in his fumbling. The dog had scant reason to love him or to seek his society. Of late, Lad had kept out of his way as much as possible. Thus it was not likely the collie had come here of his own accord, on such a night; for the mere joy of being with his tormentor.

His presence must mean that the Master was close behind; and that the whole Place was in a ferment of anxiety about the wanderer. By stoning Lad away and checking the barks, Cyril might well prevent the searchers from finding him. Too weak and too numb with cold to climb up the five-foot cliff-face to the level ground above, he did not want to miss any chance for rescue.

Hence, as Lad ceased to bark, the child set up a yell, with all his slight lung-power, to attract the seekers' notice. He ordered Lad to "Speak!" and shook his fist angrily at the dog, when no answering bark followed.

Despairing of making anyone hear his trumpeting announcement that he had found the child, Lad presently made up his mind as to the only course that remained. Wheeling about, head down, he faced the storm again; and set off at what speed he could compass, toward home, to lead the Master to the spot where Cyril was trapped. This seemed the only expedient left. It was what he had done, long ago, when Lady had caught her foot in a fox-trap, back in the woods.

As the dog vanished from against the gray-black sky-line, Cyril set up a howl of wrathful command to him to come back. Anything was better than to be in this dreary spot alone. Besides, with Lad gone, how could Lad's Master find the way to the ledge?

Twice the child called after the retreating collie. And, in another few steps, Lad had halted and begun to retrace his way toward the ledge.

He did not return because of Cyril's call. He had learned, by ugly experience, to disregard the child's orders. They were wont to mean much unpleasantness for him. Nevertheless, Lad halted. Not in obedience to the summons; but because of a sound and a scent that smote him as he started to gallop away. An eddy of the wind had borne both to the dog's acute senses.

Stiffening, his curved eyeteeth baring themselves, his hackles bristling, Lad galloped back to the ravine-lip; and stood there sniffing the icy air and growling deep in his throat. Looking down to the ledge he saw Cyril was no longer its sole occupant. Crouched at the opening of a crevice, not ten feet from the unseeing child, was something bulky and sinister;—a mere menacing blur against the darker rock.

Crawling home to its lair, supper-less and frantic with hunger, after a day of fruitless hunting through the dead forest world, a giant wildcat had been stirred from its first fitful slumber in the ledge's crevice by the impact of the child upon the heap of leaves. The human scent had startled the creature and it had slunk farther back into the crevice. The more so when the bark and inimical odor of a big dog were added to the shattering of the ravine's solitude.

Then the dog had gone away. Curiosity,—the besetting trait of the cat tribe,—had mastered the crevice's dweller. The wildcat had wriggled noiselessly forward a little way, to learn what manner of enemy had invaded its lair. And, peering out, it had beheld a spindling child; a human atom, without strength or weapon.

Fear changed to fury in the bob-cat's feline heart. Here was no opponent; but a mere item of prey. And, with fury, stirred long-unsatisfied hunger; the famine hunger of mid-winter which makes the folk of the wilderness risk capture or death by raiding guarded hencoops.

Out from the crevice stole the wildcat. Its ears were flattened close to its evil head. Its yellow eyes were mere slits of fire. Its claws unsheathed themselves from the furry pads,—long, hooked claws, capable of disemboweling a grown deer at one sabre-stroke of the muscular hindlegs. Into the rubble and litter of the ledge the claws sank, and receded, in rhythmic motion.

The compact yellow body tightened into a ball. The back quivered. The feet braced themselves. The cat was gauging its distance and making ready for a murder-spring. Cyril, his head turned the other way, was still peering up along the cliff-edge for sight of Lad.

This was what Lad's scent and hearing,—and perhaps something else,—had warned him of, in that instant of the wind's eddying shift. And this was the scene he looked down upon, now, from the ravine-lip, five feet above.

The collie brain,—though never the collie heart,—is wont to flash back, in moments of mortal stress, to the ancestral wolf. Never in his own life had Sunnybank Lad set eyes on a wildcat. But, in the primal forests, wolf and bob-cat had perforce met and clashed, a thousand times. There they had begun and had waged the eternal cat-and-dog feud, of the ages.

Ancestry now told Lad that there is perhaps no more murderously dangerous foe than an angry wildcat. Ancestry also told him a wolf's one chance of certain victory in such a contest. Ancestry's aid was not required, to tell him the mortal peril awaiting this human child who had so grievously and causelessly tormented him. But the great loyal heart, in this stark moment, took no thought of personal grudges. There was but one thing to do,—one perilous, desperate chance to take; if the child were to be saved.

The wildcat sprang.

Such a leap could readily have carried it across double the space which lay between it and Cyril. But not one-third of that space was covered in the lightning pounce.

From the upper air,—apparently from nowhere,—a huge shaggy body launched itself straight downward. As unerringly as the swoop of an eagle, the down-whizzing bulk flew. It smote the leaping wildcat, in mid-flight.

A set of mighty jaws,—jaws that could crack a beef-bone as a man cracks a filbert,—clove deep and unerringly into the cat's back, just behind the shoulders. And those jaws flung all their strength into the ravening grip.

A squall,—hideous in its unearthly clangor,—split the night silences. The maddened cat whirled about, spitting and yowling; and set its foaming teeth in the dog's fur-armored shoulder. But before the terrible curved claws could be called into action, Lad's rending jaws had done their work upon the spine.

To the verge of the narrow ledge the two combatants had rolled in their unloving embrace. Its last lurch of agony carped the stricken wildcat over the edge and out the ninety-foot drop into the ravine. Lad was all-but carried along with his adversary. He clawed wildly with his toes for a purchase on the smooth cliff wall; over which his hindquarters had slipped. For a second he hung, swaying, above the abyss.

Cyril, scared into semi-insanity by sight of the sudden brief battle, had caught up a stick from the rubbish at his feet. With this, not at all knowing what he did, he smote the struggling Lad with every atom of his feeble force, over the head.

Luckily for the gallant dog, the stick was rotten. It broke, in the blow; but not before its impact had well-nigh destroyed Lad's precarious balance.

One clawing hindfoot found toe-room in a flaw of rock. A tremendous heave of all his strained muscles; and Lad was scrambling to safety on the ledge.

Cyril's last atom of vigor and resistance had gone into that panic blow at the dog. Now, the child had flung himself helplessly down, against the wall of the ledge; and was weeping in delirious hysterics. Lad moved over to him; hesitated a moment, looking wistfully upward at the solid ground above. Then, he seemed to decide which way his duty pointed. Lying down beside the freezing child, he pressed his great shaggy body close to Cyril's; protecting him from the swirling snow and from the worst of the cold.

The dog's dark, deep-set eyes roved watchfully toward the crevice, alert for sign of any other marauder that might issue forth. His own shaggy shoulder was hurting him, annoyingly, from the wildcat's bite. But to this he gave no heed. Closer yet, he pressed his warm, furry body to the ice-cold youngster; fending off the elements as valorously as he had fended off the wildcat.

The warmth of the great body began to penetrate Cyril's numbed senses. The child snuggled to the dog, gratefully. Lad's pink tongue licked caressingly at the white face; and the collie whimpered crooning sympathy to the little sufferer.

So, for a time the dog and the child lay there; Cyril's numb body warming under the contact.

Then, at a swift intake of the windy air, Lad's whimper changed to a thunder of wild barking. His nostrils had told him of the search party's approach, a few hundred yards to the windward.

Their dispiritingly aimless hunt changing into a scrambling rush in the direction whence came the faint-heard barks, the searchers trooped toward the ledge.

"Here we are!" shrilled the child, as the Master's halloo sounded directly above. "Here we are! Down here! A—a lion tackled us, awhile back. But we licked him;—I and Laddie!"

CHAPTER VII.

THE JUGGERNAUT

Long shadows were stretching lazily athwart the lawn from the gnarled old giant trees. Over the whole drowsing world brooded the solemn hush of late summer afternoon.

An amber light hung in the sleepy air; touching with gold the fire-blue lake, the circle of lovingly protecting green hills; the emerald slope which billowed up from the water-edge to the red-roofed gray house in its setting of ancient oaks.

On the bare flooring, in the coolest corner of the veranda, two collies lay sprawled. They were fast asleep; which means that they were ready to come back to complete wakefulness at the first untoward sound.

Of the two slumbrous collies, one was slenderly graceful of outline; gold-and-white of hue. She was Lady; imperious and temperamental wisp of thoroughbred caninity.

The second dog had been crowded out of the shadiest spot of the veranda, by his mate; so that a part of his burnished mahogany coat was under the direct glare of the afternoon sun. Shimmering orange tints blazed back the reflection of the torrid light.

He was Sunnybank Lad; eighty-pound collie; tawny and powerful; with absurdly tiny white forepaws and with a Soul looking out from his deep-set dark eyes. Chum and housemate he was to his two human gods;—a dog, alone of all worshipers, having the privilege of looking on the face of his gods and of communing with them without the medium of priest or of prayer.

Lady, only, of the Place's bevy of Little People, refused from earliest puppyhood to acknowledge Lad's benevolent rulership. She bossed and teased and pestered him, unmercifully. And Lad not only let her do all this, but he actually reveled in it. She was his mate.

More,—she was his idol. This idolizing of one mate, by the way, is far less uncommon among dogs than we mere humans realize.

The summer afternoon hush was split by the whirring chug of a motor-car; that turned in from the highroad, two hundred yards beyond the house, and started down through the oak grove, along the winding driveway. Immediately, Lady was not only awake, but on her feet, and in motion. A furry gold-white whirlwind, she flashed off of the vine-shaded veranda and tore at top speed up the hill to meet the coming car.

No, it was not the Mistress and the Master whose approach stirred the fiery little collie to lightning activity. Lad knew the purr of the Place's car and he could distinguish it from any other, as far as his sensitive ears could catch its sound. But to Lady, all cars were alike; and all were signals for wild excitement.

Like too many other collies, she had a mania for rushing at any motor vehicle, and for whizzing along beside it, perilously close to its fast-moving wheels, barking and screaming hysterically and bounding upward at its polished sides.

Nor had punishment and scolding cured her of the trait. She was an addict at car-chasing. She was wholly incurable. There are such dogs. Soon or late, many of them pay high for the habit.

In early days, Lad also had dashed after motors. But a single sharp lecture from the Master had taught him that this was one of the dir- est breaches of the Place's simple Law. And, thenceforth,—though he might tremble with eagerness,—he stood statue-still when an automobile spun temptingly past him.

More,—he had cured pup after pup, at the Place, of car-chasing. But Lady he could not cure; though he never gave up the useless attempt.

Down the drive came a delivery truck; driven fast and with none too great skill. Before it had covered half the distance between gate and house, Lady was alongside. A wheel grazed her shoulder fur as, deftly, she slipped from in front of the vehicle and sprang up at its tonneau. With a ceaseless fanfare of barks,—delirious in her excite- ment,—she circled the car; springing, dodging, wheeling.

The delivery boy checked speed and shouted futile warnings to the insane collie. As he slowed down a bit on the steep grade, Lady hurled herself in front of the machine, as though taunting it for cowardice in abating its hot pace on her account.

Again and again had she run, head on, at advancing cars. It seemed to delight her when such cars slackened speed or swerved, in order not to kill her.

Now, as she whizzed backward, her vibrant muzzle a bare six inches from the shiny buffer, one of her flying feet slipped in a mud rut. Her balance gone, she tumbled.

A collie down is a collie up, in less than a second. But there was still less than a second's space between to overthrown Lady and the car's front wheels.

The boy slammed on the emergency brake. Through his mind ran the formless thought of his fate at the hands of his employer when he should return to the store with tidings that he had run over and killed a good customer's costly collie; and on the customer's own grounds.

In that single breathless instant, a huge mahogany-and-snow shape flashed forward, into the path of the machine.

Lad, following his mate, had tried to shoulder her aside and to herd her too far back from the drive for any possible return to the danger zone, until the car should have passed. More than once, at other times, had he done this. But, today, she had eluded his mighty shoulder and had flung herself back to the assault.

As she fell, she rolled over, twice, from her own momentum. The second revolution left her directly in front of the skidding wheels. One of them had actually touched her squirming spine; when white teeth gripped her by the scruff of the neck. Those teeth could crush a mutton-bone as a child cracks a peanut. But, on Lady, today, their power was exerted only to the extent of lifting her, in one swift wrench, clear of the ground and high in air.

The mischievous collie flew through space like a lithe mass of golden fluff; and came to earth, in a heap, at the edge of the drive; well clear of the menacing wheels. With Lad, it fared otherwise.

The great dog had braced himself, with all his might, for the muscle-wrenching heave. Wherefore, he had no chance to spring clear, in time to avoid the car. This, no doubt, he had realized, when he sprang to his adored mate's rescue. For Lad's brain was uncanny in its cleverness. That same cleverness, more likely than mere chance,—now came to his own aid.

The left front wheel struck him and struck him fair. It hit his massive shoulder, dislocating the joint and knocking the eighty-pound dog prone to earth, his ruff within an inch of the wheel. There was no time to gather his feet under him or to coerce the dislocated shoulder into doing its share toward lifting him in a sideways spring that should carry him out of the machine's way. There was but one thing Lad could do. And he did it.

His body in a compact bunch, he rolled midway between the wheels; making the single revolution at a speed the eye could scarce follow,—a speed which jerked him from under the impending left wheel which already had smitten him down.

Over him slid the wheel-locked car, through the mud of a recent rain; while the boy clung to the emergency brake and yelled.

Over him and past him skidded the car. It missed the prostrate dog,—missed him with all four wheels; though the rear axle's housing smeared his snowy ruff with a blur of black grease.

On went the machine for another ten feet, before it could halt. Then a chalk-faced delivery boy peered backward in fright,—to see Lad getting painfully to his feet and holding perplexedly aloft his tiny right forepaw in token of the dislocated shoulder.

The delivery boy saw more. In a swirl of black bad temper, Lady had gathered herself up from the ditch where Lad's toss had landed her. Without a moment's pause she threw herself upon the luckless dog whose rough toss had saved her life. Teeth aglint, growling ferociously, she dug her fangs into the hurt shoulder and slung her whole weight forward in the bite.

Thus was it the temperamental Lady's wont to punish real or fancied injuries from the Place's other animals,—and from humans as well, except only the Mistress and the Master. She charged first, and did her thinking afterward. Apparently, her brain, just then, could hold no impression except that her interfering mate had picked her up by the neck-scruff and had thrown her, head over heels, into a ditch. And such treatment called for instant penalty.

Under her fifty-pound impact, poor Lad's three-cornered balance gave way. Down he went in an awkward heap; while Lady snarled viciously and snapped for his momentarily exposed throat. Lad turned his head aside to guard the throat; but he made no move to resent this ungrateful onslaught; much less to fight back. Which was old Lad's way,—with Lady.

Dislocated shoulder or not, he would have flown at any male dog that assailed him; and would have made the aggressor fight for dear life. But his mate was sacred. And he merely protected his throat and let her nip agonizingly at his ears and paws; until her brief flurry of wrath should be past.

A shout from the veranda,—whither the racket had drawn the Master from his study,—put a sudden stop to Lady's brainstorm. Obedience was the first and foremost rule drilled into the Little People of the Place. And, from puppy days, the collies were taught to come,—and to come at a run,—at call from the Mistress or the Master.

Lady, with no good grace, desisted from her punitive task, and galloped down the drive to the house. Lad, rising with difficulty, followed; as fast as a three-legged gait would permit. And behind them chugged the delivery boy, bawling explanations.

A sharp word of reproof sent Lady skulking into a corner; anger forgotten in humiliation at the public rebuke. The Master paid no heed to her. Running up the drive, he met Lad, and picked up the suffering collie in his arms. Carrying him into the study, the Master gave first aid to the serious dislocation; then phoned for the nearest good vet.

As he left the study, to telephone, he encountered Lady, very woebegone and cringing, at the door. When he returned, he beheld the remorseful little gold-and-white vixen licking her mate's hurt shoulder and wagging a propitiatory tail in plea for forgiveness from the dog she had bitten and from the Master whose Law she had broken by her attack on the car.

Always, after her brief rages, Lady was prettily and genuinely repentant and eager to make friends again. And, as ever, Lad was meeting her apologies more than half-way;—absurdly blissful at her dainty attentions.

In the days that followed, Lady at first spent the bulk of her time near her lame mate. She was unusually gentle and affectionate with him; and seemed trying to make up to him for the enforced idle-ness of strained sinews and dislocated joint. In her friendliness and attention, Lad was very, very happy.

The vet had bandaged his shoulder and had anointed it with pungently smelly medicines whose reek was disgusting and even painful to the thoroughbred's supersensitive nostrils. Moreover, the vet had left orders that Lad be made to keep quiet until the hurt should heal; and that he risk no setback by undue exertion of any sort. It was sweet to lie in the Master's study,—one white forepaw or the great shapely head laid lovingly on the man's hiking boot; and with an occasional pat or a friendly word from his deity, as the latter pounded away on a clicky typewriter whose jarring noise Lad had long ago taught himself to tolerate.

Sweeter it was to be made much of and "poored" by the Mistress; and to have her light hands adjust his bandages; and to hear her tell him what a dear dog he was and praise his bravery in rescuing Lady.

Perhaps sweetest of all, in those early days of convalescence, was the amazing solicitude of Lady herself; and her queerly maternal tenderness toward him.

But, as the summer days dreamed themselves away and Lad's splendid health brought him nearer and nearer to recovery, Lady waxed restive under the long strain of indolence and of good temper. Lad had been her companion in the early morning rambles through the forest, back of the Place; in rabbit quests; in swims in the ice, cool lake at the foot of the lawn; in romps on the smooth green grass and in a dozen of the active pursuits wherein country-bred collies love to squander the outdoor days.

Less and less did Lady content herself with dull attendance on the convalescent. More and more often did she set forth without him on those cross-country runs that had meant so much to them both. Lad would watch her vanish up the drive,—their fiery little son, Wolf, cantering gleefully at her side. Then, his dark eyes full of sorrow, he would gaze at the Master and, with a sigh, would lie back on his rug—and wait.

There was something so human,—so uncomplainingly wretched,—in look and in sigh,—that the Master was touched by the big dog's loneliness and vexed at the flighty Lady's defection. Stooping down, at one such time, he ran his hand over the beautiful silky head that rested against his knee; and said in lame attempt at comfort:—

"Don't let it get under your skin, Laddie! She isn't worth it. One of your honest paws is worth more than her whole fly-away body.—Not that anyone ever was loved because he or she was worthy!—You're up against the penalty that is bound to get everybody with a soul, who is fool enough to love something or somebody without one . . . . We're going over for the mail,—the Mistress and I. Want to come along?"

At once the melancholy in Lad's deep eyes gave place to puppy-like exultance.

While, naturally, he did not understand one word in ten of the Master's frequent prosy homilies to him, or of the Mistress's more melodious speech, yet, from puppyhood, he had been talked to by both of them. And, as ever with a highbred collie, such constant conversation had borne ample fruit;—not only in giving the dog a startling comprehension of voice-meanings, but also in teaching him to understand many simple words and phrases.

For example, he recognized, as readily as would any five-year-old child, this invitation to go motoring. And it banished the memory of Lady's fickleness.

This morning, for the first time since his accident, Lad was able to spring into the car-tonneau, unaided. His hurt was all-but well. Enthroning himself in the precise center of the rear seat, he prepared to enjoy every inch of the ride.

No matter how long or how tedious were these jaunts, Lad never went to sleep or ceased to survey with eager attention the myriad details of the trip. There was something half-laughable, half-pathetic, in his air of strained interest.

Only when the Mistress and the Master both chanced to leave the car at the same time, at market or bank or postoffice, would Lad cease from this genial and absorbed inspection of everything in sight. Left alone in the machine, he always realized at once that he was on guard. Head on paws he would lie, intently scanning anyone who might chance to pause near the auto; and, with a glint of curved white fang beneath sharply upcurled lip, warning away such persons as ventured too close.

Marketing done, today, the trio from the Place started homeward. Less than a quarter-mile from their own gateway, they heard the blaring honk of a motor horn behind them.

Within a second thereafter, a runabout roared past, the cut-out making echoes along the still road; and a poisonously choking cloud of dust whirling aloft in the speedster's wake.

The warning honk had not given the Mistress time to turn out. Luckily she was driving well on her own side of the none-too-wide road. As it was, a sharp little jar gave testimony to the light touch of mudguards. And the runabout whizzed on.

"That's one of the speed-idiots who make an automobile an insult to everybody except its owner! The young fool!" stormed the Master, glowering impotently at the other car, already a hundred yards ahead; and at the back of its one occupant, a sportily-clad youth in the early twenties.

A high-pitched yelping bark,—partly of dismay, partly of warning,— from Lad, broke in on the Master's fuming remonstrance. The big dog had sprung up from his rear seat cushion and, with forepaws gripping the back of the front seat, he was peering forward; his head and shoulders between the Mistress and the Master.

Never before in all his rides had Lad so transgressed the rules of motoring behavior as to thrust himself forward like this. A word of rebuke died on the Master's tongue; as the Mistress, with a gasp of fear, pointed ahead, in the path of the speeding runabout.

Lady and Wolf had had a jolly gallop through the summer woodlands. And at last they had turned their faces homeward; for the plunge in the cool lake which was wont to follow a hot weather run. Side by side they jogged along, to the forest edge—and into the sixteen-acre meadow that stretches from forest to highway.

A few rods on the far side of the road which separated the meadow from the rest of the Place, Wolf paused to investigate a chipmunk hole. Lady was more interested just then in splashing her hot body in the chill of the lake than in exploring for hypothetical chipmunks.

Moreover, her keen ears caught a sound which rapidly swept nearer and nearer. A motor-car with the muffler cut out was approaching, at a most gratifyingly high speed.

The noise was as martial music to Lady. The speed promised exhilarating sport. Her trot merged into a headlong run; and she dashed out into the road.

The runabout was a bare fifty yards ahead of her, and it was coming on with a speed which shook even Lady's excitement-craving nerves. Here, evidently, was a playmate which it would be safer to chase than to confront head-on.

It was at this juncture, by the way, that Lad lurched forward from the rear seat and that the Mistress pointed in terror at the endangered collie.

Lady, for once overawed by speed, leaped to one side of the road. Not far, but leaving ample space for the driver to miss her by at least a yard. He had honked loudly, at sight of her. But, he had abated not an atom of his fifty-mile-an-hour pace.

Whether the man was rattled by the collie's antics,—whether he acted in sudden rage at her for startling him, whether he belonged to the filthy breed of motorist who recites chucklingly the record of his kills,—he did not hold his midroad course.

Instead,—still without checking speed,—he veered his machine slightly to the right; aiming the flying juggernaut directly
at the mischievously-poised little collie who danced in imagined
safety at the road-edge.

The rest was horror.

Merciful in its mercilessness, the hard-driven right front wheel
smote the silky golden head with a force that left no terrible
instant of fear or of agony. More lucky by far than the myriad
innocent and friendly dogs that are left daily to scream out their
lives writhingly in the wake of speeding motor-cars, Lady was
killed at a single stroke.

The fluffy golden body was hurled far in front of its slayer; and
the wheels struck it a second time. The force of the impact caused
the runabout to skid, perilously; and the youthful driver brought
it to a jarring and belated halt. Springing to the ground, he rolled
the dead collie's impeding body into the shallow wayside ditch,
clear of his wheels. Then, scrambling aboard again, he jammed
down the accelerator.

Lad had made a flying leap over the door of the Master's car.
He struck ground with a force which crumpled his healing right
shoulder under him. Heedless of the pain, he hurled himself
forward, on three legs, at an incredible speed; straight for the
runabout. His great head low, his formidable teeth agleam beneath drawn-back lips, his soft eyes a-smolder with red flame,
Lad charged.

But, for all his burst of speed, he was too late to avenge; even
as he had been too late to save. By the time he could reach the
spot where Lady lay crumpled and moveless in the ditch, the
runabout had gathered full speed and was disappearing down
the bend of the highway.

After it flew Lad, silent, terrible,—not stopping to realize that
the fleetest dog,—even with all four of his legs in commission,—
cannot hope to overhaul a motor-car driven at fifty miles an hour.

But, at the end of a furious quarter-mile, his wise brain took charge once more of his vengeance-craving heart. He halted, snarled hideously after the vanished car, and limped miserably back to the scene of the tragedy.

There, he found the Mistress sitting in the roadside dust, Lady's head in her lap. She was smoothing lovingly the soft rumpled fur; and was trying hard not to cry over the inert warm mass of gold-and-white fluffiness which, two minutes earlier, had been a beautiful thoroughbred collie, vibrant with life and fun and lovableness.

The Master had risen from his brief inspection of his pet's fatal injuries. Scowling down the road, he yearned to kick himself for his stupidity in failing to note the Juggernaut's number.

Head and tail a-droop, Lad toiled back to where Lady was lying. A queer low sound, strangely like a human sob, pulsed in his shaggy throat, as he bent down and touched his dead mate's muzzle with his own. Then, huddling close beside her, he reverted all at once to a trait of his ancestors, a thousand generations back.

Sitting on his haunches and lifting his pointed nose to the summer sky, he gave vent to a series of long-drawn wolf howls; horrible to hear. There was no hint of a housebred twentieth century dog in his lament. It was the death-howl of the primitive wolf;—a sound that sent an involuntary shiver through the two humans who listened aghast to their chum's awesome mourning for his lost mate.

The Master made as though to say something,—in comfort or in correction. The Mistress, wiser, motioned to him not to speak.

In a few seconds, Lad rose wearily to his feet; the spasm of primal grief having spent itself. Once more he was himself; sedate, wise, calm.

Limping over to where the car had halted so briefly, he cast about the ground, after the manner of a bloodhound.

Presently, he came to an abrupt halt. He had found what he sought. As motionless as a bird-dog at point, he stood there; nose to earth, sniffing.

"What in blazes—?" began the Master, perplexed.

The Mistress was keener of eye and of perception. She understood.

She saw the Lad's inhalingly seeking muzzle was steady above a faint mark in the road-dust;—the mark of a buckskin shoe's print. Long and carefully the dog sniffed. Then, with heavy deliberation he moved on to the next footprint and the next. The runabout's driver had taken less than a half dozen steps in all; during his short descent to the ground. But Lad did not stop until he had found and identified each and every step.

"He knows!" marveled the Mistress. "He saw the brute jump down from his car. And he has found his footsteps. He'll remember them, too."

"Little good it will do the poor chap!" commented the Master. "He can't track him, that way. Get aboard, won't you?" he went on. "I'll make Lad go back into the tonneau again, too. Drive down to the house; and take Lad indoors with you. Better telephone to the vet to come over and have another look at his shoulder. He's wrenched it badly, in all that run. Anyway, please keep him indoors till—"

He finished his sentence by a glance at Lady. At the Master's order, Lad with sore reluctance left the body of his mate; whither he had returned after his useless finding of the footmarks. He had just curled up, in the ditch, pressing close to her side; and again that unnatural sobbing sound was in his throat. On the Master's bidding, Lad crossed to the car and suffered himself to be lifted aboard. The Mistress started down the drive. As they went, Lad ever looked back, with suffering despair in his dark eyes, at that huddle of golden fur at the wayside.

The Master carried the pitifully light armful to a secluded spot far beyond the stables; and there he buried it. Then, satisfied that Lad could not find his mate's grave, he returned to the house.

His heart was heavy with helpless wrath. Again and again, in the course of their drives, he and the Mistress had sickened at sight of mutely eloquent little bodies left in mid-road or tossed in some ditch,—testimony to the carelessness and callous hoggishness of autoists. Some few of these run-over dogs,—like poor Lady,—had of course tempted fate; spurred on by that strange craving which goaded them to fly at cars. But the bulk of them had been strolling peacefully along the highways or crossing to or from their own dooryards, when the juggernauts smashed them into torture or into instant death.

The Master reflected on the friendly country folk who pay taxes for the scenery and for the fine roads which make motoring so pleasant;—and on the reward so many motorists bestow upon these rural hosts of theirs by wanton or heedless murder of pet animals. For the first time, he could understand how and why farmers are tempted to strew glass or tacks in the road to revenge the slaying of a beloved dog.

For the next few days, until his shoulder was again in condition to bear his eighty-pound weight on it, Lad was kept indoors or on the veranda. As soon as he was allowed to go out alone, the big collie went straight to the spot where last he had seen Lady's body. Thence, he a made a careful detour of the Place,—seeking for—something. It was two days before he found what he sought.

In the meantime,—as ever, since his mate's killing,—he ate practically nothing; and went about in a daze.

"He'll get over it presently," prophesied the Master, to soothe his wife's worry.

"Perhaps so," returned the Mistress. "Or perhaps not. Remember he's a collie, and not just a human."

On the third day, Lad's systematic quartering of the Place brought him to the tiny new mound, far beyond the stables. Twice, he circled it. Then he lay down, very close beside it; his mighty head athwart the ridge of upflung sod.

There,—having seen him from a distance,—the Master came across to speak to him. But at sight of the man, the collie got up from his resting place and moved furtively away.

Time after time, during the next week, the Master or the Mistress found him lying there. And always, at their approach, he would get up and depart. Nor did he go direct to the mound, on these pilgrimages; but by devious paths; as though trying to shake off possible pursuit.

No longer did he spend the nights, as from puppyhood, in his beloved "cave" under the piano in the music room. On one pretext or another, he would manage to slip out of the house, during the evening. Twice, in gray dawn, the Master found him crouched beside the mound, where, sleepless, he had lain all night.

The Mistress and the Master grew seriously troubled over their collie chum's continued grief. They thought, more than once, of sending him away to boarding kennels or to some friend, for a month or two; to remove him from the surroundings which made him so wretched. Oddly enough, his heartbreak struck neither of them as absurd.

They had made a long study of collie nature in all its million queer and half-human phases. They knew, too, that a grieving dog is upheld by none of the supports of Faith nor of Philosophy; and that he lacks the wisdom which teaches the wondrous anaesthetic powers of Time. A sorrowing dog sorrows without hope.

Nor did Lad's misery seem ridiculous to the Place's many kindly neighbors; with whom the great dog was a favorite and who were righteously indignant over the killing of Lady.

Then in a single minute came the cure.

On Labor Day afternoon, the finals in a local tennis tournament were to be played at the mile distant country club. The Mistress and the Master went across to the tournament; taking Lad along. Not that there could be anything of the remotest interest to a dog in the sight of flanneled young people swatting a ball back and forth. But Lad was a privileged guest at all outdoor functions; and he enjoyed being with his two deities.

Thus, when the two climbed the clubhouse veranda, Lad was at their heels; pacing along in majestic unhappiness and not turning his beautiful head in response to any of a dozen greetings flung at him. The Mistress found a seat among a bevy of neighbors. Lad lay down, decorously, at her feet; and refused to display the faintest interest in anything that went on around him.

The playing had not yet begun. New arrivals were drifting up the steps of the clubhouse. Car after car disgorged women in sport clothes and men in knickerbockers or flannels. There was plenty of chatter and bustle and motion. Lad paid no heed to any of it.

Then, up to the foot of the veranda steps jarred a flashy runabout; driven by a flashier youth. At word from the policeman in charge he parked his car at the rear of the clubhouse among fifty others, and returned on foot to the steps.

"That's young Rhuburger," someone was confiding to the Mistress. "You must have read about him. He was arrested as a Conscientious Objector, during the war. Since then, his father has died, and left him all sorts of money. And he is burning it; in double handfuls. No one seems to know just how he got into the club, here. And no one seems to—"

The gossipy maundering broke off short; drowned in a wild beast growl.

Both the Mistress and her husband had been eyeing Rhuburger as he ascended the veranda steps in all the glory of unbelievably exquisite and gaudy raiment. There seemed to both of them something vaguely familiar about the fellow; though neither could place him. But, to Lad, there was nothing at all vague in his recollections of the gorgeous newcomer.

As Rhuburger reached the topmost step, the collie lifted his head, his nostrils dilating wide. A thrill went through him. His nearsighted eyes swept the crowd. They rested at last on Rhuburger. Another deep inhalation told him all he needed to know. Not in vain had Lad sniffed so long and so carefully at those faint footprints in the road dust, at the spot where Lady died. In his throat a deep growl was born.

"Hello, folks!" Rhuburger was declaiming, to a wholly unenthusiastic circle of acquaintances. "Made another record, just now. The little boat spun me here from Montclair in exactly nineteen minutes. That's—that's roughly an average rate of a mile in seventy-five seconds. Not so bad, eh? That car sure made a hit with *me*, all right. Not so much of a hit, maybe, with a couple of chickens and a fat old dog that had the bad luck to be asleep in the middle of the—"

His plangent brag was lost in a sound seldom heard on the hither side of jungle or zoo. From the group of slightly disgusted onlookers, a huge and tawny shape burst forth; hurtling through the air, straight for the fat throat of the boaster.

Rhuburger, by some heaven-sent instinct, flung up his arms to shield his menaced jugular. He had no time to do more.

Lad's fury-driven eighty pounds of muscular weight crashed full against his chest. Lad's terrible teeth, missing their throat-goal, drove deep into the uplifted right forearm; shearing through imported tweed coat-sleeve and through corded silken shirt, and through flabby flesh and clean to the very bone.

The dog's lion-roar blended with the panic-screeches of the victim. And, under that fearful impact, Rhuburger reeled back from the stairhead, and went crashing down the steps, to the broad stone flagging at the bottom.

Not once, during that meteoric, shriek-punctured downward flight, did Lad loose his grip on the torn forearm. But as the two struck the flagging at the bottom, he shifted his hold, with lightning speed; stabbing once more for the exposed jugular.

He lunged murderously at his mark. Yes, and this time he found it. His teeth had touched the pudgy throat, and began to cleave their remorseless way to the very life of the man who had slain Lady.

But, out of the jumble of cries and stamping feet and explosive shouts from the scared onlookers on the veranda above, one staccato yell pierced the swirl of rage-mists in the avenging collie's brain.

"*Lad!*" came the Master's sharp, scandalized mandate. "*LAD!!!*"

Hating the thought of desisting from his cherished revenge, the dog heard and heeded. With visible reluctance, he drew back from the slaughter; and turned his noble head to face the man who was running down the steps toward him.

Lad knew well what he might expect, for this thing he had

done. He knew the Law. He knew, almost from birth, the courteous tolerance due to folk among whom his deities took him. And
now he had made an industrious effort to kill one of these people.

It was no light offense for a dog to attack a human. Lad, like
every well-trained collie, knew that. His own death might well
follow. Indeed, from the babel of voices on the veranda, squalling
confusedly such hackneyed sentiments as "Mad dog!" and "Get
a gun!" it seemed highly probable that Lad was due to suffer full
penalty, from the man-pack.

Yet he gave no heed to the clamor. Instead, turning slowly, he
faced the Master; ready for whatever might follow. But nothing
followed,—nothing at least that he expected.

The Master simply commanded:—

"Down, Lad!"

As the dog, obediently, dropped to the ground, the Master bent
to examine the groaning and maudlinly weeping Rhuburger. In
this Samaritan task he was joined by one or two of the club's more
venturesome members who had followed him down the steps.

Rhuburger was all-but delirious with fright. His throat was
scored by the first raking of Lad's teeth; but in the merest of
flesh-wounds. The chewed arm was more serious; but no bone
or tendon was injured. A fortnight of care would see it as good
as new. By more or less of a miracle, no bones had been broken
and no concussion caused by the backward dive down the flight
of steps. There were bad bruises a-plenty; but there was nothing
worse.

As the Master and the few others who had descended the
steps were working over the fallen man, the Mistress checked the
turmoil on the veranda. At Lad's leap, memory of this speed-mad
motorist had rushed back to her.

Now, tersely, for the benefit of those around, she was iden-
tifying him with the killer of Lady; whose death had roused so
much indignation in the village. And, as she spoke, the people
who had clamored loudest of mad dogs and who had called so

frantically for a gun, waxed silent. The myriad glances cast at the prostrate and blubbering Rhuburger were not loving. Someone even said, loudly:

"*GOOD* old Laddie!"

As the Mistress and the Master were closing the house for the night, a car came down the drive. Out of it stepped their friend of many years, Maclay, the local Justice of the Peace.

"Hello, Mac!" hailed the Master. "Here to take us all to jail for assault-and-battery; or just to serve a 'dangerous dog' notice on us?"

He spoke lightly; but he was troubled. Today's escapade might well lead the village law to take some cognizance of Lad's ferocious deed.

"No," laughed Maclay. "Neither of those things. I'm here, unprofessionally. I thought you people might like to know a few things, before you go to bed. In the first place, the doctor patched up Rhuburger's bites and took him home. He couldn't take him home in Rhuburger's own car. For some of the tennis crowd had gotten at that. What they did to that $6,000 runabout was a crime! They stripped it of everything. They threw the carburetor and the wheels and the steering gear and a lot of other parts into the lake."

"*What?*"

"Then they left their cards pinned to the dismantled machine's cushions;—in case Rhuburger cares to go further into the matter. While they were doing all that, the club's Governors had a hurry-call meeting. And for once the Board was unanimous about something. It was unanimous—in expelling Rhuburger from the club. Then we—By the way, where's Laddie? Curled up by Lady's grave, as usual, I suppose? Poor old dog!"

"No," denied the Mistress. "He's asleep in his 'cave' under the piano. He went there, of his own accord. And he ate a perfectly tremendous supper, tonight. He's—he's *cured!*"

CHAPTER VIII.

IN STRANGE COMPANY

L ad was getting along in years.

Not yet had age begun to claw at him; blearing the wondrous deep-set dark eyes and silvering the classic muzzle and broadening the shapely skull and stiffening the sweepingly free gait; dulling the sharp ears or doing any of the other pitiably tragic things that nature does to the dog who is progressing in his teens. Those, humiliations were still waiting for Lad, one by one; beyond the next Turn of the Road.

Yet the romp and the spirit of bubbling fun and the lavishly needless exercise—these were merging into sobriety. True, at rare times, with the Mistress or the Master—especially with the Mistress, Lad would forget he was middle-aged and dignified; and would play like a crazy puppy. But, for the most part he had begun to carry his years a trifle seriously.

He was not yet in the winter or even the Indian Summer of his beautiful life. But, at least, he had strolled into its early autumn.

And this, be it well remembered, is the curse which Stepmother Nature placed upon The Dog, when he elected to turn his back on his own kind, and to become the only one of the world's four-footed folk to serve Man of his own accord. To punish the Dog for this abnormality, Nature decreed that his life should begin to fail, almost as soon as it had reached the glory of its early prime.

A dog is not at his best, in mind or in body, until he has passed his third year. And, before he nears the ten-year mark, he has begun to decline. At twelve or thirteen, he is as decrepit as is the average human of seventy. And not one dog in a hundred can be expected to live to fourteen.

(Lad, by some miracle, was destined to endure past his own sixteenth birthday; a record seldom equaled among his race.)

And so to our story:—

When the car and the loaded equipment-truck drew up at the door, that golden October day, Lad forgot his advancing years. In a moment, he was once more a puppy. For he knew what it all meant. It did not need the advent of the Mistress and the Master from the house, in rough outing clothes, nor the piling of duffle-bags and the like into the car's tonneau, to send Laddie into a transport of trumpeting and gyrations. The first sight and sniff of the tents, rolled tight in the truck, had done that. Lad understood. Lad always understood.

This gear meant the annual fall camping trip in the back reaches of the Ramapo Mountains, some twenty-odd miles north of the Place; the fortnight of tent-life, of shooting, of fishing, of bracingly chill nights and white-misted dawns and of drowsily happy campfire evenings. It meant all manner of adventure and fun for Lad.

Now, on a fishing jaunt, the presence of any kind of dog is a liability; not an asset. A thousand dog-fancier fishermen can attest to that. And, when humans are hunting any sort of game, a collie is several degrees worse than worthless.

Thus, Lad's usefulness, as a member of the party, was likely to be negligible;—except in the matter of guarding camp and as an all-round pal for the two campers.

Yet, as on former years, there was no question of leaving him at home. Where the Mistress and the Master went, he went, too; whenever such a thing were possible. He was their chum. And they would have missed him as much as he would have missed them.

Which, of course, was an absurd way for two reasonably sane people to regard a mere dog. But, then, Lad was not a "mere" dog.

Thus it was that he took his place, by invitation, in the car's tonneau, amid a ruck of hand-luggage; as the camp-ward pilgrimage began. Ten miles farther on, the equipment truck halted to take aboard a guide named Barret, and his boy; and their professionally reliable old Irish setter.

This setter had a quality, not over-common with members of his grand breed; a trait which linked his career pathetically with that of a livery-plug. He would hunt for anybody. He went through his day's work, in stubble or undergrowth, with the sad conscientiousness of an elderly bookkeeper.

Away from the main road, and up a steadily rising byway that merged into an axle-snapping mountain-track, toiled the cars; at last coming to a wheezy and radiator-boiling halt at the foot of a rock-summit so steep that no vehicle could breast it. In a cup, at the summit of this mountain-top hillock, was the camp-site; its farther edge only a few yards above a little bass-populated spring-lake.

The luggage was hauled, gruntily, up the steep; and camp was pitched. Then car and truck departed for civilization. And the two weeks of wilderness life set in.

It was a wonderful time for old Lad. The remoteness and wild stillness of it all seemed to take him back, in a way, to the wolf-centuries of his ancestors. It had been monstrous pleasant to roam the peaceful forest back of the Place. But there was a genuine thrill in exploring these all-but manless woods; with their queer scents of wild things that seldom ventured close to the ordained haunts of men.

It was exciting, to wake at midnight, beside the smoldering campfire, and to hear, above the industrious snoring, of the guide and his boy, the stealthy forest noises; the pad-pad-pad of some wary prowler circling at long range the twinkling embers; the crash of a far-off buck; the lumbering of some bear down to the lake to drink. The almost moveless sharp air carried a myriad fascinating scents which human nostrils were too gross to register; but which were acutely plain and understandable to the great dog.

Best of all, in this outing, Lad's two deities, the Mistress and the Master, were never busy at desk or piano, or too much tangled up with the society of silly outsiders, to be his comrades and playmates. True, sometimes they hurt his supersensitive feelings most distressingly, by calling to him: "No, no, Laddie. Back! Watch camp'" when he essayed to join them as they set forth with rods over their shoulders for a half-day's fishing; or as, armed with guns, they whistled up the bored but worthy setter for a shooting trip. But, for the most, Lad was close at their sides, during these two wonderful weeks. And he was very happy.

Once, during a solitary ramble, before the humans had awakened in the morning, Lad caught an odd scent; and followed it for a quarter mile down the mountainside. It waxed stronger and ranker. At last, a turn around a high boulder brought him face to face with its source. And he found himself confronting a huge black bear.

The bear was busy looting a bee-tree. It was the season when he and his like are stocking up, with all the fatmaking food they can gorge, in preparation for the winter's "holing-in." Thus, he viewed with sluggish non-interest the advent of the dog. He had scented Lad for as long a time as Lad had scented him. But he had eaten on, unperturbed. For he knew himself to be the match of any four dogs; especially if the dogs were unaccompanied by men. And, a long autumn of food had dulled his temper.

So, he merely checked his honey-gorging long enough to roll a rotted log to one side and to scoop up from under it a pawful of fat white grubs which had decided to winter beneath the decayed trunk. Then, absent-mindedly brushing aside a squadron of indignant bees, he continued his sweet feast.

As Lad rounded the boulder and came to a growling halt, the bear raised his honey-smeared head, showed a yellowing fang from under one upcurled corner of his sticky lips; and glowered evilly at the collie from out of his reddening little eyes. Then he made as though to go on eating.

But Lad would not have it so. Into his rejuvenated heart stole a tinge of the mischief which makes a collie puppy dash harrowingly at a tethered cow. Barking with sheer delight in the excitement of meeting this savage-looking monster, the dog rushed merrily at the bear. His teeth were not bared. His hackles were not bristling. This was no fight; but a jolly game. Lad's dark eyes danced with fun.

Midway of his charge, he checked himself. Not through fear, but from utter astonishment. For his new acquaintance had done a right non-quadrupedal thing. Bruin had reared himself upon his hind legs; and was standing there, like a man, confronting the dog. He towered, thus, ever so high above Lad's head.

His short arms, with their saber-shaped claws, were outstretched toward Lad, as if in humble supplication. But there was nothing supplicating or even civil in the tiny red eyes that squinted ferociously down at the collie. Small wonder that Laddie halted his own galloping advance; and stood doubtful!

The Master, a minute earlier, had turned out of the blankets for his painfully icy morning plunge in the lakelet. The fanfare of barking, a quarter-mile below, changed his intent. A true dogman knows his dog's bark,—and its every shade of meaning,—as well as though it were human speech. From the manner wherewith Lad had given tongue, the Master knew he had cornered or treed something quite out of the common. Catching up his rifle, he made for the direction of the bark; running at top speed.

The bear put an end to the moment of hesitancy. Lunging forward, he raked at the crouching collie, with one of his murderous claws; in a gesture designed to gather the impudent dog into his death-embrace.

Now, even from humans, except only the Mistress and the Master, Lad detested patting or handling of any kind. Whether he thought this maneuver of the bear's an uncouth form of caress or knew it for a menace,—he moved back from it. Yet he did so with a leisurely motion, devoid of fear and expressive of a certain lofty contempt. Perhaps that is why he moved without his native caution.

At all events, the tip of one of the sweeping claws grazed his ear, opening the big vein, and hurting like the very mischief.

On the instant, Lad changed from a mischievous investigator to a deeply offended and angry dog. No longer in doubt as to Bruin's intent, he slithered out of reach of the grasping arms, with all the amazing speed of a wolf-descended collie of the best sort. And, in practically the same fraction of a second, he had flashed back to the attack.

Diving in under the other's surprisingly agile arms, he slashed the bear's stomach with one of his razorlike eyeteeth; then spun to one side and was out of reach. Down came the bear, on all fours; raging from the slash. Lurching forward, he flung his huge bulk at the dog. Lad flashed out of reach, but with less leeway than he would have expected. For Bruin, for all his awkwardness, could move with bewildering speed.

And, as the bear turned, Lad was at him again, nipping the hairy flank, till his teeth met in its fat; and then diving as before under the lunging body of the foe.

It was at this point the Master hove in sight. He was just in time to see the flank-bite and to see Lad dance out of reach of the furious counter. It was an interesting spectacle, there in the gray dawn and in the primeval forest's depths;—this battle between a gallant dog and a ragingly angry bear. If the dog had been other than his own loved chum, the Master might have stood there and watched its outcome. But he was enough of a woodsman to know there could, in all probability, be but one end to such a fight.

Lad weighed eighty pounds,—an unusually heavy weight for a collie that carries no loose fat,—and he was the most compactly powerful dog of his size the Master had ever seen. Also, when he chose to exert it, Lad had the swiftness of a wildcat and the battling prowess of a tiger.

Yet all this would scarce carry him to victory, or even to a draw, against a black bear several times heavier than himself and with the ability to rend with his claws as well as with his teeth. Once let Lad's foot slip, in charge or in elusive retreat,—once let him misjudge time or distance—and he must be crushed to a pulp or ripped to ribbons.

Wherefore, the Master brought his rifle to his shoulder. His finger curled about the trigger. But it was no easy thing, by that dim light, to aim with any accuracy. Nor was there the slightest assurance that Lad,—dancing in and out and everywhere and nowhere at once,—might not come in line with the bullet. Thus,—from a tolerable knowledge of bears and of their comparative mildness in the plump season of the year,—he shouted at the top of his lungs; and, at the same time, fired into the air.

The bluff sufficed. Even as Lad jumped back from close quarters and whirled about, at sound of the voice and the shot,—the bear dropped to all fours, with ridiculous haste; and shambled off at very creditable speed into the tangle of undergrowth.

Not so far gone in the battle-lust had Bruin been that he cared to risk conflict with an armed man. Twice, before, in his somewhat long life, had he heard at close quarters the snap of a rifle, in the forest stillness, and the whine of a bullet. Once, such a bullet had found its mark by scoring a gouge on his scalp; a gouge which gnats and mayflies and "no-see-'ems" and less cleanly pests had made a torment for him, for weeks thereafter.

Bruin had a good memory. Just now, he had nothing to defend. He was not at bay. Nor had the fight-fury possessed him to the exclusion of sanity. Thus, he fled. And, eagerly, Lad gave chase.

But, at the very edge of the bush-rampart, the Master's call brought the collie back, to heel, exceeding glum and reluctant. Reproachfully, Lad gazed up at the man who had spoiled his morning of enthralling sport. Halfheartedly, Lad listened to the Master's rebuke, as he followed back to camp. His day had begun so delightfully! And, as usual, a human had interrupted the fun, at the most exciting time; and for no apparent reason. Humans were like that.

Barring one other incident, Lad's two weeks at camp were uneventful,—until the very last day. That "one incident" can be passed over, with modest brevity. It concerned a black-and-white cat which Lad saw, one evening, sneaking past the campfire's farthest shadows. He gave chase. The chase ended in less than ten seconds. And, Lad had to be bathed and scoured and rubbed and anointed, for the best part of twenty-four hours, before he was allowed to come again within fifty feet of the dining tent.

On a raw morning, the car and the truck made their appearance at the foot of the rocky mountaintop hillock. The tents had been struck, at daylight; and every cooking utensil and dish had been scoured and put into the crate as soon as it was used. Camp was policed and cleaned. The fire was beaten to death; a half-score pails of water were dowsed over its remains; and damp earth was flung upon it.

In short, the camping spot was not only left as it had been found and as one would want it to be found again, but every trace of fire was destroyed.

And all this, be it known, is more than a mere rule for campers. It should be their sacred creed. If one is not thoroughgoing sportsman enough to make his camp-site scrupulously clean, at least there is one detail he should never allow himself to neglect;—a detail whose omission should be punished by a term in prison: Namely, the utter extinction of the campfire.

Every year, millions of dollars' worth of splendid trees and of homes are wiped out, by forest fires. No forest fire, since the birth of time, ever started of its own accord. Each and every one has been due to human carelessness.

A campfire ill-extinguished;—a smolder of tobacco not stamped out;—the flaming cinders of a railroad train,—a match dropped among dry leaves before spark and blaze have both been destroyed,— these be the first and only causes of the average forest fire. All are avoidable. None is avoided. And the loss to property and to life and to natural resources is unbelievably great.

Any fool can start a forest fire. Indeed, a fool generally does. But a hundred men cannot check it. Forest wardens post warnings. Forest patrols, afoot or in airships, keep sharp watch. But the selfish carelessness of man undoes their best precautions.

Sometimes in spring or in lush summer, but far oftenest in the dry autumn, the Red Terror stalks over mountain and valley; leaving black ruin in its wake. Scarce an autumn passes that the dirty smoke reek does not creep over miles of sweet woodland, blotting out the sunshine for a time and blotting out rich vegetation for much longer.

This particular autumn was no exception. On the day before camp was broken, the Mistress had spied, from the eyrie heights of the knoll, a grim line of haze far to southward; and a lesser smoke-smear to the west. And the night sky, on two horizons, had been faintly lurid.

The campers had noted these phenomena, with sorrow. For, each wraithlike smoke-swirl meant the death of tree and shrub. Lad noted the smudges as distinctly as did they. Indeed, to his canine nostrils, the chill autumn air brought the faint reek of wood-smoke; an odor much too elusive, at that distance, for humans to smell. And, once or twice, he would glance in worried concern at these humans; as if wondering why they took so coolly a manifestation that a thousand-year-old hereditary instinct made the dog shrink from.

But the humans showed no outward sign of terror or of rage. And, as ever, taking his tone from his gods, Lad decided there was nothing to fear. So, he tried to give no further heed to the reek.

The driver of the truck and his assistant were full of tales of the fire's ravages in other sections. And their recital was heard with active interest by the folk who for fourteen days had been out of touch with the world.

"It's well we're lighting out for civilization," said the Master, as he superintended the loading of the truck. "The woods are as dry as tinder. And if the wind should change and grow a bit fresher, the blaze over near Wildcat Mountain might come in this direction. If ever it does, it'll travel faster than any gang of fire-fighters can block it. This region is dead ripe for such a thing. Not a drop of rain in a month . . . . No, no, Laddie!" he broke off in his maunderings, as the collie sought to leap aboard the truck in the wake of a roll of bedding. "No, no. You're going with us, in the car."

Now, long usage and an uncanny intelligence had given Lad a more than tolerable understanding of the English language's simpler phrases. The term, "You're going with us in the car," was as comprehensible to him as to any child. He had heard it spoken, with few variations, a thousand times, in the past nine years. At once, on hearing the Master's command, he jumped down from the truck; trotted off to the car, a hundred yards distant; and sprang into his wonted place in the luggage-cluttered tonneau.

He chanced to jump aboard, from one side; just as the guide's hobbledehoy son was hoisting a heavy and cumbersome duffle bag into the tonneau, from the other. Lad's eighty pounds of nervous energy smote the bag, amidships; as the boy was balancing it high in air, preparatory to setting it down between two other sacks. As a result, boy and bag rolled backward in a tangled embrace, across several yards of stony ground.

Lad had not meant to cause any such catastrophe. Yet he stood looking down in keen enjoyment at the lively spectacle. But as the boy came to a halt, against a sharp-pointed rock, and sat up, sniveling with pain, the great dog's aspect changed. Seeming to realize he was somehow to blame, he jumped lightly down from the car and went over to offer to the sufferer such comfort as patting forepaw and friendly licking tongue could afford.

"Here!" called the guide, who had seen but a crosssection of the collision. "Here, you! Stop a-playin' with the dorg, and hustle them bags onto—"

"I wa'n't playin' with him," half-blubbered the boy, glowering dourly at the sympathetic Lad; and scrambling up from his bruise-punctured roll on the ground. "He came a-buntin' me; and I—"

"That'll do, Sonny!" rasped Barret, who was strong on discipline and who fancied he had witnessed the climax of a merry game between boy and dog, "I seen what I seen. And I don't aim to take no back-talk from a wall-eyed, long-legged, chuckle-headed brat; that's hired to help his poor old dad and who spends his time cuttin' monkeyshines with a dorg. You take that collie over to the truck, and ask his boss to look after him and to see he don't pester us while we're aworkin'. On the way back, stop at the lean-to and catch me that bag of cookin' things I left there. The's just room for 'em, under the seat. Chase!"

Woefully, the boy limped off; his hand clinched in the fur of Lad's ruff. The dog, ordinarily, would have resented such familiarity. But, still seeking to comfort the victim's manifest unhappiness, he suffered himself to be led along. Which was Lad's way. The sight of sorrow or of pain always made him ridiculously gentle and sympathetic.

The boy's bruises hurt cruelly. The distance to the truck was a full hundred yards. The distance to the lean-to (a permanent shed, back of the camp-site) was about the same, and in almost the opposite direction. The prospect of the double journey was not alluring. The youth hit on a scheme to shorten it. First glancing back to see that his father was not looking, he climbed the bare stony hillock, toward the lean-to; Lad pacing courteously along beside him.

Arrived at the shed, he took from a nail a rope-length; tied it around Lad's neck; fastened the dog to one of the uprights; shouldered the cooking-utensil bag; and started back toward the car.

He had saved himself, thus, a longer walk; and had obeyed his father's orders to take Lad away. He was certain the Master, or one of the others, missing the dog, would see him standing forlornly there, just outside the lean-to's corner; or that another errand would bring some of the party to the shed to release him. At best, the boy was sore of heart and of body, at his own rough treatment. And he had scant interest anything else.

Twenty minutes later, the truck chugged bumpily off, upon its trip down the hazardous mountain track. The guide's boy rode in triumph on the seat beside the truckman;—a position of honor and of excitement.

"Where's Lad?" asked the Mistress, a minute afterward, as she and the Master and the guide made ready to get into the car and follow.

"Aboard the truck," responded Barret, in entire good faith. "Him and my boy got a-skylarkin' here. So I sent Bud over to the truck with him."

"That's queer!" mused the Mistress. "Why, Laddie never condescends to play,—or 'skylark,' as you call it,—with anyone except my husband or myself! He—"

"Never mind!" put in the Master. "We'll catch up with the truck before it's gone a mile. And we can take Laddie aboard here, then. But I wonder he consented to go ahead, without us. That isn't like Lad. Holiday-spirits, I suppose. This trip has made a puppy of him. A stately old gentleman like Laddie would never think of rounding up bears and skunks, if he was at home." As he talked, the car got under way; moving at rackety and racking "first speed" over hummock and bump; as it joggled into the faint wheeltrack. By reason of this noise and of the Master's stupid homily, none of the trio heard an amazed little bark, from the knoll-top, a hundred yards behind them.

Nor did the car catch up with the truck. At the end of the first half mile, the horrible roadbed began to take toll of the elderly tires. There were two punctures, in rapid succession. Then came a blowout. And, at the bottom of the mountain a third puncture varied the monotony of the ride. Thus, the truck reached the Place well ahead of the faster vehicle.

The Mistress's first question was for Lad. Terror seized upon the guide's boy, as he remembered where he had left the dog. He glanced obliquely at the truckman, who had unloaded and who was cranking.

"Now—" said the scared youth, glibly, avoiding his father's unsuspecting eye. "Now—now, Lad he was settin' 'twixt Simmons and me. And he hops down and runs off around the house, towards— towards the lake—soon as we stopped here. Most likely he was thirsty-like, or something."

The Mistress was busy with details of the car's unpacking. So she accepted the explanation. It seemed probable that the long and dusty ride should have made Lad thirsty; and that after his drink at the lake, he had made the rounds of the Place; as ever was his wont after his few brief absences from home.

Not until dinnertime did she give another thought to her loved pet's absence. The guide and his boy had long since departed, on the truck, for their ten-mile distant home. Nor, even yet, did it occur to the Mistress to question the truth of the youngster's story. She merely wondered why, for the first time in his life, Lad should absent himself at dinnertime from his time-honored place on the dining-room floor, at the Master's left. And, amusedly, she recalled what her husband had said of the stately dog's new propensity for mischief. Perhaps Lad was exploring the friendly home-woods in search of a bear!

But when ten o'clock came and Lad did not seek the shelter of his "cave" under the music-room piano, for the night, there was real worry. The Mistress went out on the veranda and sounded long and shrilly upon the silver whistle which hung from her belt.

From puppyhood, Laddie had always come, at a sweeping gallop, on sound of this whistle. Its notes could travel, through still air, for a half mile or more. Their faintest echoes always brought the dog in eager response. But tonight, a dozen wait-punctuated blasts brought no other response than to set the distant village dogs to barking.

The Mistress went back into the house, genuinely worried. Acting on a sudden idea, she called up the Place's superintendent, at the gatelodge.

"You were down here when the truck came to the house this afternoon, weren't you?" she asked.

"Yes, ma'am," said the man. "I was waiting for it. Mike and I helped Simmons to unload."

"Did you see which way Lad went, when he jumped out of the truck?" pursued the Mistress. "Or have any of you seen him since then?"

"Why, no, ma'am," came the puzzled answer. "I haven't seen him at all. I supposed he was in the car with you, and that maybe he'd been in the house ever since. He wasn't on the truck: That's one sure thing. I saw it stop; and I stayed till they finished emptying it. Lad wasn't there."

There was a moment's pause. Then, the Mistress spoke again. Her voice slightly muffled, she said:

"Please find out if there is plenty of gas in my car;—enough to take it—say, forty miles. Thank you."

"What on earth—?" began the Master, as his wife left the telephone and picked up an ulster.

"Laddie didn't come home on the truck," she made tremulous reply. "And he wasn't with us. He hasn't come home all."

"He'll find his way, easily enough," returned the Master, albeit with no great assurance. "Lad's found his way farther than that. He—"

"If he was going to find his way," interrupted the Mistress, "he'd have found it before now. I know Laddie. So do you. He is up there. And he can't get back. He—"

"Nonsense!" laughed the Master. "Why, of course, he—"

"He is up there," insisted the Mistress, "and he can't get back. I know him well enough to be, sure he'd have overtaken us, when we stopped all those times to fix the tires;—if he had been left behind. And I know something else: When we started on, after that first puncture, we were about half a mile below the knoll. And as we went around the bend, there was a gap in the trees. I was looking back. For a second, I could see the lean-to, outlined ever so clearly against the sky. And alongside of it was standing some animal. It was far away; and we passed out of sight so suddenly, that I couldn't see what it was; except that it was large and dark. And it seemed to be struggling to move from where it stood. I was going to speak to you about it,—I supposed it was that black bear of Laddie's,—when we had the next puncture. And that made me forget all about it;—till now. Of course, it never occurred to me it could be Lad. Because Barret had said he was in the truck. But—but oh, it *was* Laddie! He—he was fastened, or caught, in some way. I know he was. Why, I could see him struggle to—"

"Come on!" broke in the Master, hustling into his mackinaw. "Unless you'll stay here, while I—"

"No," she protested. "I'm going. And I'm going because I'm thinking of the same thing that's troubling you. I'm thinking of those forest fires and of what you said about the wind changing and—"

"Come on!" repeated the Master; starting for the garage.

Which shows how maudlinly foolish two otherwise sane people can be; when they are lucky enough to own such a dog as Sunnybank Lad. Naturally, the right course, at so cold and late an hour of the autumn night, and after a long day of packing and motoring and unpacking, was to go to bed; and to trust to luck that the wise old collie would find his way back again. Instead, the two set off on a twenty-mile wildgoose chase, with worried faces and fast-beating hearts. It did not occur to either of them to stay at home; or to send someone else on the long, frosty drive in search of the missing dog.

Lad had watched the preparations for departure with increasing worry. Also, the abnormally sensitive old fellow was wretchedly unhappy. Except at dog-shows, he had never before been tied up. And at such shows, the Mistress and the Master were always on hand to pet and reassure him. Yet, here, he had suffered himself to be tied by a smelly rope to the rotting post of a lean-to, by a comparative stranger. And, in the open ground below the hillock, his deities moved back and forth without so much as an upward glance at him.

Then, to his dismay, truck and car had made off down the mountainside; and he had been left alone in his imprisonment. Except for a single unheard bark of protest, Lad made no effort to call back the departing humans. Never before had they forsaken him. And he had full trust that they would come back in a few minutes and set him free.

When the car halted, a half-mile below, Lad felt certain his faith was about to be justified. Then, as it moved on again, he sprang to the end of his short rope, and tried to break free and follow.

Then came the dying away of the chugging motor's echoes; and silence rolled up and engulfed the wilderness hilltop.

Lad was alone. They had gone off and left him. They had with never a word of goodby or a friendly command to watch camp until their return. This was not the dog's first sojourn in camp. And his memory was flawless. Always, he recalled, the arrival and the loading of the truck and the striking of tents had meant that the stay was over and that at the party was going home.

Home! The charm and novelty of the wilderness all at once faded. Lad was desperately lonely and desperately unhappy. And his feelings were cruelly hurt; at the strange treatment accorded him.

Yet, it did not occur to him to seek freedom and to follow his gods to the home he loved. He had been tied here, presumably by their order; certainly with their knowledge. And it behooved him to wait until they should come to release him. He knew they would come back, soon or late. They were his gods, his chums, his playmates. They would no more desert him than he would have deserted them. It was all right, somehow. Only, the waiting was tedious!

With a tired little sigh, the collie curled up in a miserable heap on the stony ground, the shortness of his tether making even this effort at repose anything but comfortable. And he waited.

A dog, that is happy and well, settles himself for a prolonged wait, by stretching out on his side;—oftenest the left side; and by dropping off into slumber. Seldom, unless he be cold or ill, does a big dog curl up into a ball, to rest. Nor is he thoroughly comfortable in such a posture.

Lad was not comfortable. He was not resting. He was wretched. Nor did he try to snooze. Curled in a compact heap, his sorrowful eyes abrim with sorrow, he lay scanning the bumpy mountainside and straining his ears, for sign of the car's return. His breathing was not as splendidly easy as usual. For, increasingly, that earlier twinge of acrid smoke-reek was tickling his throat. The haze, that had hovered over the farther hilltops and valleys, was thickening; and it was creeping nearer. The breath of morning breeze was stiffening into a steady wind; a wind that blew strong from the west and carried on it the smell of forest fire.

Lad did not enjoy the ever-stronger smoke scent. But he gave only half-heed to it. His main attention was centered on that winding wagon-track whence the car and the truck had vanished into the lowlands. And, through the solemnly spent hours he lay forlornly watching it.

But, after sunset, the smoke became too pervasive to be ignored longer. It was not only stinging his throat and lungs, but it was making his eyes smart. And it had cut off the view of all save the nearer mountain-peaks.

Lad got to his feet; whining softly, under his breath. Ancestral instinct was fairly shouting to his brain that here was terrible peril. He strained at his thick rope; and looked imploringly down the wagon-road.

The wind had swelled into something like a gale. And, now, to Lad's keen ears came the far-off snap and crack of a million dry twigs as the flame kissed them in its fast-crawling advance. This sharper sound rose and fell, as a theme to the endless and slowly-augmenting roar which had been perceptible for hours.

Again, Laddie strained at his heavy rope. Again, his smoke-stung eyes explored the winding trail down the mountain. No longer was the trail so distinguishable as before. Not only by reason of darkness, but because from that direction came the bulk of the eddying gusts of wind-driven smoke.

The fire's mounting course was paralleling the trail; checked from crossing it only by a streambed and an outcrop of granite which zigzagged upward from the valley. The darkness served also to tinge the lowering sky to south and to westward with a steadily brightening lurid glare. The Master had been right in his glum prophecy that a strong and sudden shift of wind would carry the conflagration through the tinder-dry undergrowth and dead trees of that side of the mountain, far faster than any body of fire-fighters could hope to check it.

The flame-reflection began to light the open spaces below the knoll, with increasing vividness. The chill of early evening was counteracted waves of sullen heat, which the wind sent swirling before it.

Lad panted; from warmth as much as from nervousness. He had

gone all day without water. And a collie, more perhaps than any other dog, needs plenty of fresh, cool water to drink; at any and all times. The hot wind and the smoke were parching his throat. His thirst was intolerable.

Behind him, not very many yards away, was the ice-cold mountain lakelet in which so often he had bathed and drunk. The thought of it made him hate the stout rope.

But he made no serious effort to free himself. He had been tied there,—supposedly by the Master's command. And, as a well-trained dog, it was his place to stay where he was, until the Master should free him. So, apart from an instinctive tug or two at his moorings, he submitted to his fate.

But, in mid-evening, something occurred, to change his viewpoint, in this matter of nonresistance.

The line of fire, climbing the mountain toward him, had encountered a marshy stretch; where, in normal weather, water stood inches deep. Despite the drought, there was still enough moisture to stay the advance of the red line until the dampness could be turned to dust and tindery vegetation. And, in the meanwhile, after the custom of its kind, the fire had sought to spread to either side. Stopped at the granite-outcrop to the right, it had rolled faster through the herbage to the left.

Thus, by the time the morass was dry enough for the flame to pass it, there was a great sickle of crawling red fire to the left; which encircled a whole flank of the mountain and which was moving straight upward.

Lad knew nothing of this; nor why the advance of the fire's direct line had been so long checked. Nor did he know, presumably, that this sickle of flame was girdling the mountain-flank; like a murderous net; hemming in all live things within the flaming arc and forcing them on in panic, ahead of its advance. Perhaps he did not even note the mad scurryings in undergrowth and bramble, in front of the oncoming blaze. But one thing, very speedily, became apparent to him:—

From out a screen of hazel and witch-elm (almost directly in front of the place where the truck, that morning, had been loaded) crashed a right hideous object. By sight and by scent Lad knew the creature for his olden foe, the giant black bear.

Growling, squealing, a dozen stinging fiery sparks sizzling through his bushy coat, the bear tore his way from the hedge of thicket and out into the open. The fire had roused him from his snug lair and had driven him ahead of it with a myriad hornets of flame, in a crazed search for safety.

At sight of the formidable monster, Lad realized for the first time the full extent of his own helplessness. Tethered to a rope which gave him scarce twenty-five inches of leeway, he was in no fit condition to fend off the giant's assault.

He wasted no time in futile struggles. All his race's uncanny powers of resource came rushing to his aid. Without an instant's pause, he wheeled about; and drove his keen teeth into the rope that bound him to the post.

Lad did not chew aimlessly at the thick tether; nor throw away one ounce of useless energy. Seizing the hempen strands, he ground his teeth deeply and with scientific skill, into their fraying recesses. Thus does a dog, addicted to cutting his leash, attack the bonds which hold him.

It was Lad's first experience of the kind. But instinct served him well. The fact that the rope had been left out of doors, in all weathers, for several years, served him far better. Not only did it sever the more easily; but it soon lost the cohesion needed for resisting any strong pull.

The bear, lurching half-blindly, had reeled out into the open, below the knoll. There, panting and grunting, he turned to blink at the oncoming fire and to get his direction. For perhaps a half-minute he stood thus; or made little futile rushes from side to side. And this breathing space was taken up by Lad in the gnawing of the rope.

Then, while the collie was still toiling over the hempen mouthfuls, the bear seemed to recover his own wonted cleverness; and to realize his whereabouts. Straight up the hillock he charged, toward the lean-to; his splay feet dislodging innumerable surface stones from the rocky steep; and sending them behind him in a series of tiny avalanches.

Lad, one eye ever on his foe, saw the onrush. Fiercely he redoubled his efforts to bite through the rope, before the bear should be upon him. But the task was not one to be achieved in a handful of seconds.

Moving with a swiftness amazing for an animal of his clumsy bulk, the bear swarmed up the hillock. He gained the summit; not three yards from where Laddie struggled. And the collie knew the rope was not more than half gnawed through. There was no further time for biting at it. The enemy was upon him.

Fear did not enter the big dog's soul. Yet he grieved that the death-battle should find him so pitifully ill-prepared. And, abandoning the work of self-release, he flung himself ragingly at the advancing bear.

Then, two things happened. Two things, on neither of which the dog could have counted. The bear was within a hand's breadth of him; and was still charging, headlong. But he looked neither to right nor to left. Seemingly ignorant of Lad's presence, the huge brute tore past him, almost grazing the collie in his insane rush; and sped straight on toward the lake beyond.

That was one of the two unforeseen happenings. The other was the snapping of the rotted rope, under the wrench of Lad's furious leap.

Free, and with the severed rope's loop still dangling uselessly from around his shaggy throat, the dog stood staring in blank amaze after his former adversary. He saw the bear reach the margin of the icy lake and plunge nose deep into its sheltering waters. Here, as Bruin's instinct or experience had foretold, no forest fire could harm him. He need but wallow there until the Red Terror should have swept past and until the scorched ground should be once more cool enough to walk on.

Lad turned again toward the slope. He was free, now, to follow the wagon track to the main road and so homeward, guided perhaps by memory, perhaps by scent; most probably guided by the mystic sixth sense which has more than once enabled collies to find their way, over hundreds of miles of strange territory, back to their homes.

But, in the past few minutes, the fire's serpent-like course had taken a new twist. It had flung volleys of sparks across the upper reach of granite rock-wall, and had ignited dry wood and brier on the right hand side of the track. This, far up the mountain, almost at the very foot of the rock-hillock.

The way to home was barred by a three-foot-high crackling fence of red-gold flame; a flame which nosed hungrily against the barren rocks of the knoll-foot; as if seeking in ravenous famine the fuel their bare surfaces denied it.

And now, the side of the hillock showed other signs of forest life. Up the steep slope thundered a six-antlered buck, snorting shrilly in panic and flying toward the cool refuge of the little lake.

Far more slowly, but with every tired muscle astrain, a fat porcupine was mounting the hill; its claws digging frantically for foothold among the slippery stones. It seemed to flow, rather than to run. And as it hurried on, it chuckled and scolded, like some idiot child.

A bevy of squirrels scampered past it. A long snake, roused from its stony winter lair, writhed eerily up the slope, heedless of its fellow travelers' existence. A raccoon was breasting the steep, from another angle. And behind it came clawing a round-paunched opossum; grinning from the pain of sparks that were stinging it to a hated activity.

The wilderness was giving up its secrets, with a vengeance. And the Red Terror, as ever, was enforcing a truce among the forest-folk; a truce bred of stark fear. One and all—of those that had been aroused in time to get clear of the oncoming fiery sickle—the fugitives were making for the cool safety of the lake.

Lad scarce saw or noted any of his companions. The road to home was barred. And, again, ancestral instinct and his own alert wit came to his aid. Turning about, and with no hint of fear in his gait or in the steady dark eyes, he trotted toward the lake.

Already the bear had reached its soothing refuge; and was standing hip deep in the black waters; now and then ducking his head and tossing showers of cold spray over his scorched shoulder-fur.

Lad trotted to the brink. There, stooping—not fifty feet away from Bruin—he lapped thirstily until he had at last drunk his fill. Then, looking back once in the direction of the fire-line, he lay down, very daintily indeed, in shallow water; and prepared to enjoy his liberty. Scourged by none of the hideous fear which had goaded his fellow fugitives, he watched with grave interest the arrival of one after another of the refugees; as they came scurrying wildly down to the water.

Lad was comfortable. Here, the smoke-reek stung less acutely. Here, too, were grateful darkness, after the torrid glare of the fire, and cold water and security. Here were also many diverting creatures to watch. It would have been pleasant to go home at once. But, since that was out of the question, there were far worse things than to lie interestedly at ease until the Master should come for him.

The fire raged and flickered along the base of the bare rocky knoll; and, finding no path of advance, turned back on itself, fire-fashion; seeking new outlet. The thin line of bushes and other undergrowth at the hillock's foot were quickly consumed; leaving only a broad bed of ember and spark. And the conflagration swept on to the left, over the only course open to it. To the right, the multiple ridges of rock and the dearth of vegetation were sufficient "No Thoroughfare" enforcement.

This same odd rock-formation had kept the wagon track clear, up to the twist where it bore to leftward at the base of the knoll. And the Mistress and the Master were able to guide their rattlingly protesting car in safety up the trail from the main road far below. The set of the wind prevented them from being blinded or confused by smoke. Apart from a smarting of the eyes and a recurrent series of heat waves, they made the climb with no great discomfort;—until the final turn brought them to an abrupt halt at the spot where the wide swath of red coals and flaming ashes marked the burning of the hillock foot bushes.

The Master jumped to earth and stood confronting the lurid stretch of ash and ember with, here and there, a bush stump still crackling merrily. It was not a safe barrier to cross; this twenty-foot-wide fiery stretch. Nor, for many rods in either direction, was there any way around it.

"There's one comfort," the Master was saying, as he began to explore for an opening in the red scarf of coals, "the fire hasn't gotten up to the camp-site. He—"

"But the smoke has," said the Mistress, who had been peering vainly through the hazecurtain toward the summit. "And so has the heat. If only—"

She broke off, with a catch in her sweet voice. And, scarce realizing what she did, she put the silver whistle to her lips and blew a piercingly loud blast.

"What's that for?" asked the Master, crankily, worry over his beloved dog making his nerves raw. "If Lad's alive, he's fastened there. You say you saw him struggling to get loose, this morning. He can't come, when he hears that whistle. There's no sense in—How in blue blazes he ever got fastened there,—if he really was,—is more than I can—"

"Hush!" begged the Mistress, breaking in on his grumbled monologue. "Listen!"

Out of the darkness, beyond the knoll-top, came the sound of a bark,—the clear trumpeting welcome-bark which Lad reserved for the Mistress and the Master, alone; on their return from any absence.

Through the night it echoed, gaily, defiantly; again and again; ringing out above the obscene hiss and crackle and roar of the forest-fire. And at every repetition, it was nearer and nearer the dumfounded listeners at the knoll foot.

"It's—it's Laddie!" cried the Mistress, in wondering rapture. "Oh, it's *Laddie!*"

The Master, hearing the glad racket, did a thoroughly asinine thing. Drawing in his breath and holding his coat in front of him, he prepared to make a dash through the wide smear of embers, to the hilltop; where, presumably, Lad was still tied. But, before he could take the first step, the Mistress stayed him.

"Look!" she cried, pointing to the hither side of the knoll; lividly bright in the ember-glow.

Down the steep was galloping at breakneck speed a great, tawny shape. Barking rapturously,—even as he had barked when first the whistle's blast had roused him from his lazy repose in the lakeside shallows,—Lad came whizzing toward the two humans who watched so incredulously his wild approach.

The Master, belatedly, saw that the collie could not avoid crashing into the spread of embers; and he opened his mouth to order Lad back. But there was not time.

For once, the wise dog took no heed of even the simplest caution. His lost and adored deities had called him and were awaiting him. That was all Lad knew or cared. They had come back for him. His horrible vigil and loneliness and his deadly peril were ended.

Too insanely happy to note where he was treading, he sprang into the very center of the belt of smoldering coals. His tiny white forefeet—drenched with icy water—did not remain among them long enough to feel pain. In two more bounds he had cleared the barrier and was dancing in crazy excitement around the Mistress and the Master; patting at them with his scorched feet; licking their eagerly caressing hands; "talking" in a dozen different keys of rapture, his whimpers and growls and gurgles running the entire gamut of long-pent-up emotions.

His coat and his feet had, for hours, been immersed in the cold water of the lake. And, he had fled through the embers at express-train speed. Scarce a blister marked the hazardous passage. But Lad would not have cared for all the blisters and burns on earth. His dear gods had come back to him,—even as he had known they would!

Once more,—and for the thousandth time—they had justified his divine Faith in them. Nothing else mattered.

CHAPTER IX.

OLD DOG; NEW TRICKS

A mildewed maxim runs: "You can't teach an old dog new tricks." Some proverbs live because they are too true to die. Others endure because they have a smug sound and because nobody has bothered to bury them. The one about old dogs and new tricks belongs in both categories. In a sense it is true. In another it is not.

To teach the average elderly dog to sit up and beg, or to roll over twice, or to do other of the asinine things with which humans stultify the natural good sense of their canine chums, is as hard as to teach a sixty-year-old grave-digger to become a musical composer.

But no dog with a full set of brains is ever past learning new things which are actually needful for him to learn. And, sad to say, many an old dog, on his own account, picks up odd new accomplishments—exploits which would never have occurred to him in his early prime. Nobody knows why. But it has happened, numberless times.

And so it was with Sunnybank Lad.

Laddie had passed his twelfth birthday; when, by some strange freak, he brought home one day a lace parasol. He had found it in the highroad, on his way back to the Place after a sedate ramble in the forest. Now, it was nothing new for the great collie to find missing articles belonging to the Mistress or to the Master. Every now and then he would lay at their feet a tobacco pouch or a handkerchief or a bunch of keys that had been dropped, carelessly, somewhere on the grounds; and which Lad recognized, by scent, as belonging to one of the two humans he loved.

These bits of treasure trove, he delighted in finding and restoring. Yes, and—though those who had never seen him do this were prone to doubt it—he was certain to lay the recovered object at the feet of whichever of the two had lost it. For instance, it never occurred to him to drop a filmy square of lace-and-cambric at the muddied feet of the Master; or a smelly old tobacco-pouch at the Mistress's little feet.

There was nothing miraculous about this knowledge. To a high-bred dog, every human of his acquaintance has a distinctive scent; which cannot be mistaken. Lad used no occult power inn returning to the rightful owner any article he chanced to find on lawn or on veranda.

But the lace parasol was different. That, presumably, had fallen from some passing motor-car, bound for Tuxedo or for the Berkshires. It did not belong at the Place.

Lad happened to see it, lying there in the highway. And he brought it, forthwith, to the house; carrying it daintily between his mighty jaws; and laying it on the living-room floor in front of the astonished Mistress. Probably, he laid it before her, instead of before the Master, because she was the first of the two whom he happened to encounter. It is doubtful if he realized that a parasol is a purely feminine adjunct;—although the Mistress always declared he did.

She picked up the gift and looked it over with real admiration. It was a flimsily beautiful and costly thing; whose ivory handle was deftly carven and set with several uncut stones; and whose deep fringe of lace was true Venetian Point.

"Why, Laddie!" she exclaimed, in wondering delight. "Where in the world did you get this? Look!" she went on, as her husband came in from his study. "See what Laddie brought me! I saw him coming down the drive with something in his mouth. But I had no idea what it was. Isn't it a beauty? Where do you suppose he—?"

"As long as motorists go around curves at forty miles an hour," decided the Master, "so long their piled-up valuables are likely to be jostled out of the tonneau. I found a satchel, last week, at the curve, up there, you remember; and a hat, the week before. What are you going to do about this thing?"

"Oh," said the Mistress, with a sigh of renunciation, "I suppose we'll have to advertise it; and watch the 'Lost and Found' columns, too. But—wouldn't it be glorious if nobody should see our advertisement or—or ever advertise for it? It's so lovely! I hate to think it may belong to somebody who can't appreciate it as I do."

Now, Laddie had lived on the Place for many more years than he could remember. And he had spent the bulk of that time in studying the faces and the voices and the moods of these two people whom he worshiped. Moreover, he had an intelligence that is not given to most dogs,—even to collies—and a queer psychic twist to his brain that had puzzled his owners as much as it had delighted them:

Watching the Mistress, now, with his classic head on one side and his deep-set dark eyes fixed on her eager face, he saw that his roadway gift had made her very happy. Also, that her caressing hand on his head showed pride in what he had done. And this, as ever, thrilled the old dog, to the very soul.

He wagged his plumed tail, in gladness, and thrust his nose into her palm and began to "talk" in gleeful treble. To none but the Mistress and the Master would Lad deign to "talk." And, none listening to him could doubt he was trying to copy the human voice and human meanings.

"Dear old Laddie!" praised the Mistress, running her fingers through his lion-like ruff. "*Good* Laddie! Thank you, ever so much! Nobody but a very, *very* wonderful collie named Lad could have had the perfect taste to pick out such a parasol. And now we're going to have a whole handful of animal crackers, for reward."

The crooningly sweet voice, the petting, the gift of animal crackers of which he was childishly fond—all these delighted Lad beyond measure. And they confirmed him in the belief that he had done something most laudable.

What he had done was to pick up a stray object, away from home, and bring it to the Mistress. He knew that. And that was all he knew. But, having won high praise for the deed, he resolved then and there to repeat it.

Which proves that old dogs can be taught new tricks. And which started all the trouble.

That afternoon, the Mistress and the Master went for a five-mile ramble through the woods and over the mountains, back of the Place. With them went old Laddie, who paced gravely between them. With them, also, went Bruce, the magnificent dark sable collie of kingly look and demeanor; who was second only to Lad in human traits and second to no living animal in beauty. Bruce was glorious to look upon. In physique and in character he had not a flaw. There was a strange sweetness to his disposition that I have found in no other dog.

With Lad and Bruce, on this walk, raced Lad's fiery little golden son, Wolf.

Of old, Lad had led such runs. Now, advancing age and increased weight had begun to make him chary of throwing away his fading energies. Wherefore, he walked between his two deities; and let the two younger dogs do the galloping and rabbit chasing.

And he had his reward. For, as they neared the highroad on the way home, Wolf and Bruce chanced to tree a squirrel. Thus, Lad was first to reach the road with the two humans. Suddenly, he darted ahead of them; and snatched up from the wayside the somewhat worn case of a thermos bottle which had been discarded there or had fallen from a car-seat. This he bore to the Mistress; fairly vibrating with pride in his own exploit.

Noting his joy in the deed, she made much of the shabby gift; praising and thanking Lad, inordinately; and forbearing to throw away the worn case until the collie was out of sight.

Of late, as Laddie began to show signs of age, she and the Master had taken to making more and more of him; to atone for his growing feebleness and to anticipate the dark day which every dog-owner must face;—the day when his voice and his caress can no longer mean anything to the pet who once rejoiced so utterly in them.

All of which went to confirm Lad in the natural belief that

anything found on the road and brought to the Mistress would be looked on with joy and would earn him much gratitude. So,—as might a human in like circumstances,—he ceased to content himself with picking up trifles that chanced to be lying in his path, in the highway, and fell to searching for such flotsam and jetsam.

He began the hunt, next morning. Pacing gravely along the center of the road, he headed toward the mile-distant village. By sheer luck, such few automobiles as chanced along, at that hour, were driven by folk who had heart enough to slow down or to turn aside for the majestically strolling old dog. To the end of his long life, Lad could never be made to understand that he was not entitled to walk at will in the exact middle of the road. Perhaps his lofty assurance in taking such a course made motorists check speed to spare him.

This morning, he had fared but a half-mile when he saw a car drawn up at the edge of the road, beside a shaded bit of turf. Several people had just descended from it; and were making preparations for an early picnic lunch. One of them had finished depositing a basket on the ground, at the side of the car farthest from the strip of sward where the others were spreading a sea-rug and setting an impromptu table.

The man put the basket down in the road. Then he dived back into the nether regions of the machine for more provender. And he was engaged in this groping when Lad came in view, around a bend.

The big collie saw the basket standing there, unprotected and, so far as he knew, ownerless. Gravely he stepped forward, lifted the heavy receptacle by the handle and turned about with it; still moving with dignified slowness. The table-setters were busy; and the car was between him and them.

By the time the other member of the party succeeded in finding the things he was seeking under the rear seat, Lad had rounded the bend and was out of sight. To this day, none of the motorists has the remotest solution to the mystery of the vanished lunch.

Lad had not stolen the basket. He would have suffered himself to be cut in three, before sinking to theft or to any other sneaking act. He had found a basket standing alone in the highroad, several feet away from the nearest humans. He had no way of guessing it belonged to them. So far as he was concerned, this was as much a lost article as had been the gorgeous parasol. He had been praised to the skies for bringing the parasol and the thermos case to the Mistress. He had every reason to expect the same meed of praise for this new gift.

Indeed, to Lad's way of thinking, he might well hope for even higher praise. For the parasol had been an odorless and foolish thing of no apparent usefulness; while this basket exhaled most heavenly scents of fried chicken and other delectable foods. Heavy as was the burden, it did not occur to Lad to set it down. Fragrant as were its contents, it did not occur to him to nose the cover off and sample them. There was no tinge of snooping in his make-up. No, the basket was a gift for the Mistress. And as such he was bearing it home to her.

"See what Laddie brought me, this time!" cried the Mistress, coming into her husband's study, a few minutes later, and holding forth the trophy. "It's full of food, too; and of course he never touched a mouthful of it. But I gave him two of the frosted cakes, by way of reward. He's ridiculously happy over them,—and over the fuss I made about the basket."

"H'm!" mused the Master, inspecting the present. "Jostled off the car-seat, as some fool of a driver took the curve at top speed! Well, that same driver has paid for his recklessness, by the loss of his lunch. It's funny, though—There's not a trace of mud or dust on this; and even the food inside wasn't jostled about by the tumble. That curve is paying us big dividends, lately. It's a pity no bullion trucks pass this way. Still, parasols and picnic lunches aren't to be sneered at."

Lad was standing in the study doorway, eyes alight, tail waving. The Master called him over and petted him; praising this newest accomplishment of his, and prophesying untold wealth for the Place if the graft should but continue long enough.

There was something pathetic in dear old Laddie's pleasure over the new trick he had learned; or so it seemed to the two people who loved him. And they continued to flatter him for it;—even when, among other trophies, he dragged home a pickaxe momentarily laid aside by a road mender; and an extremely dead chicken which a motor-truck wheel had flattened to waferlike thickness.

Which brings us, by degrees to the Rennick kidnaping case.

Claude Rennick, a New York artist of considerable means, had rented for the summer an ancient Colonial farmhouse high among the Ramapo hills; some six miles north of the Place, There, he and his pretty young wife and their six-months-old baby had been living for several weeks; when, angered at a sharp rebuke for some dereliction in his work, Schwartz, their gardener, spoke insultingly to Mrs. Rennick.

Rennick chanced to overhear. Being aggressively in love with his wife, he did not content himself with discharging Schwartz. Instead, he thrashed the stalwart gardener, then and there; and ended the drastic performance by pitching the beaten man, bodily, out of the grounds.

Schwartz collected his battered anatomy and limped away to his home in the hills just above. And, that night, he called into council his two farmhand brothers and his wife.

Several characteristic plans of revenge were discussed in solemn detail. These included the burning of the Rennick house or barn, or both; the shooting of Rennick from among the hillside boulders as the artist sketched; of waylaying him on his walk to the post-office, by night, and crippling him for life; and other suggestions equally dear to the hearts of rural malefactors.

But one plan after another was vetoed. To burn any of the property would cause Rennick nothing worse than temporary annoyance; as he merely rented the farm. Daylight shooting was a dangerous and uncertain job; especially since automobiles had opened up the district to constantly passing outsiders. It was Schwartz himself who decided against waylaying his foe by night. He had too recent memories of Rennick's physical prowess to care about risking a second dose of the same medicine. And so on with the other proposals. One and all were rejected.

Then it was that Mrs. Schwartz hit upon an idea which promised not only punishment, but profit. She had done washing for the Rennicks and she had access to the house. She proposed that they steal the Rennick baby, on the first night when opportunity should offer; carry him to a car the brothers were to have waiting; and thence take him to her sister in Paterson.

There, the youngster would be well cared for. In a family of not less than seven children, the presence of an extra baby would not excite police query. Her sister had more than once taken babies to board with her, during their mothers' temporary absence in service or in jail. And the newcomer could pass readily as one of these.

Negotiations could set in; and, if care were taken, a reward of at least two thousand dollars might be extracted safely from the frantic parents. Thus, the Rennicks could be made to sweat blood and money too, in payment of the injuries wrought upon the aching frame of Schwartz. At first, the three men sheered off from the plan. Kidnaping is a word with an ugly sound. Kidnaping is a deed with ugly consequences. Kidnaping is a crime whose perpetrators can hope for no atom of sympathy from anybody. Kidnaping is perilous, past words.

But, deftly, Mrs. Schwartz met and conquered the difficulties raised. In the first place, the baby would come to no harm. Her sister would see to that. In the second, the matter of the reward and of the return could be juggled so as to elude detectives and rural constables. She had known of such a case. And she related the details;—clever yet utterly simple details, and fraught with safety to all concerned;—details which, for that very reason, need not be cited here.

Bit by bit, she went on with her outline of the campaign; testing each step and proving the practicability of each.

The next Thursday evening, Rennick and his wife went, as usual, to the weekly meeting of a neighborhood bridge club which they had joined for the summer. The baby was left in charge of a competent nurse. At nine o'clock, the nurse went to the telephone in reply to a call purporting to be from an attendant at a New York hospital.

This call occupied the best part of twenty minutes. For the attendant proceeded to tell her in a very roundabout way that her son had been run over and had come to the hospital with a broken leg. He dribbled the information; and was agonizingly long-winded and vague in answering her volley of frightened questions.

Shaken between duty to her job and a yearning to catch the next train for town, the nurse went back at last to the nursery. The baby's crib was empty.

It had been the simplest thing in the world for Mrs. Schwartz to enter the house by the unfastened front door, while one of her husband's brothers held the nurse in telephone talk; and to go up to the nursery, unseen, while the other servants were in the kitchen quarters. There she had picked up the baby and had carried him gently down to the front door and out of the grounds.

One of Schwartz's brothers was waiting, beyond the gate; with a disreputable little runabout. Presently, the second brother joined him. Mrs. Schwartz lifted the baby into the car. One of the men held it while the other took his place at the steering wheel. The runabout had started upon its orderly fourteen-mile trip to Paterson, before the panic stricken nurse could give the alarm.

Mrs. Schwartz then walked toward the village, where her husband met her. The two proceeded together to the local motion picture theater. There, they laughed so loudly over the comedy on the screen that the manager had to warn them to be quieter. At once, the couple became noisily abusive. And they were ordered ignominiously from the theater. There could scarcely have been a better alibi to prove their absence of complicity in the kidnaping.

Meanwhile, the two brothers continued quietly on their journey toward Paterson. The baby slept. His bearer had laid him softly on the floor of the car. A few drops of paregoric, administered by Mrs. Schwartz as the child awoke for an instant on the way to the gate, insured sound slumber. The joggling of the car did not rouse the tiny sleeper; as he lay snugly between the feet of the man into whose care he had been given.

The first six miles of the easy journey were soon traversed. Then, with a pop and a dispiritedly swishing sound, a rear tire collapsed. Out into the road jumped both men. Their nerves were none too steady. And, already, in fancy they could hear all the police cars in New Jersey close at their heels. It behooved them to change tires in a hurry, and to finish their nerve-twisting trip.

The driver vaulted over the side nearest him and began to explore the under-seat regions for a jack. The other man picked up the baby and hurried to the rear of the runabout to detach the spare tire from its dusty rack. Manifestly, he could not unstrap the tire while he was carrying a baby in his arms. So he set down his burden at the roadside, near him.

Then, still obsessed by fear of pursuit, he hit on a safer scheme. Picking up the sleeper again, he carried the warm little bundle to the far side of the road, some thirty yards beyond, and deposited it there, behind a dwarf alder bush which screened it from any stray automobilist who might be passing. Thus, in case of pursuit, he and his brother would merely be changing tires; and would know nothing of any missing baby.

Failing to find a jack under the seat, the driver climbed over into the adjoining field in search of two or three big stones to serve the same purpose in holding up the axle. For several minutes the men worked fast and tensely; blind and deaf to anything except the need of haste.

Thus it was that neither of them saw a tawny-and-snow collie,— huge and shaggy except for a pair of absurdly tiny white forepaws,— come pacing majestically along the road from the direction in which they were heading. The car lamps played but faintly upon the advancing Lad; for the dimmers had been applied.

The big dog was taking his usual before-bedtime stroll. Of old, that evening stroll had been confined to the Place's grounds, a quarter-mile beyond. But, lately, his new obsession for finding treasures for the Mistress had lured him often and oftener to the highway.

Tonight, as for a day or so past, he had drawn blank in his quest. The road had been distressingly bare of anything worth carrying home. But, now, as he moved along, his near-sighted eyes were attracted by a dim blur of white, behind a bush, at the road-edge; just within the dim radiance of the car-lamps. Even sooner than he saw this, his keen nostrils had told him of human presence there. He shifted his course to investigate.

Standing over the compactly-fastened swathing of clothes, Laddie bent down and sniffed. It was a human. He knew that; in spite of the thick veil that covered the slumberer's face. But it was also a bundle. It was a bundle which might well be expected to delight the Mistress almost as much as had the parasol;—far more than had the defunct chicken.

Daintily, with infinite gentleness, Lad fixed his teeth in the loosest portion of the bundle that he could find; and lifted it. It was amazingly heavy, even for so powerful a dog. But difficulties had never yet swerved Lad from any set purpose. Bracing his strength, he turned homeward, carrying the burden between his mighty jaws.

And now, he was aware of some subtler feeling than mere desire to bring the Mistress one more gift. His great heart had ever gone out in loving tenderness toward everything helpless and little. He adored children. The roughest of them could take unpardonable liberties with him. He would let them maul and mistreat him to their heart's content; and he reveled in such usage; although to humans other than the Mistress and the Master, he was sternly resentful of any familiarity.

His senses told him this bundle contained a child;—a baby. It had been lying alone and defenseless beside the road. He had found it. And his heart warmed to the helpless little creature which was so heavy to carry.

Proudly, now, he strode along; his muscles tensed; moving as if on parade. The bundle swinging from his jaws was carried as lovingly as though it might break in sixty pieces at any careless step.

The spare tire was adjusted. The men glanced nervously up and down the road. No car or pedestrian was in sight. The driver scrambled to his place at the wheel. His brother crossed to the alder bush behind whose shelter he had left the baby. Back he came, on the run.

"'Tain't there!" he blithered. "'Tain't there! 'Tain't rolled nowheres, neither. It's been took! Lord! What're we goin' to—?"

He got no further. His brother had scrambled down from the seat; and pushed him aside, in a dash for the alder. But a few seconds of frantic search proved the baby was gone. The two men glared at each other in silent horror. Then by tacit impulse they got into the car.

"It couldn't 'a' walked off, could it?" gurgled the driver. "They can't walk, can they;—not at six months? Not far, anyhow?"

"It—it was took!" sputtered his brother between chattering teeth.

Another moment of scared silence. Then the driver rallied his awed faculties. Stepping on the self-starter, he brought the runabout into motion, and headed down the road.

"Where are you goin'?" queried the other. "No use a-keepin' on, this d'rection. It—"

"If it was took," answered the driver, truculently, "'twasn't took by no car. We'd 'a' heard a car or we'd 'a' saw it. If it had been took by two or three folks a-walkin', we'd 'a' heard 'em blat to each other when they seen the kid layin' there. That means it was took by one person, all alone. He didn't pass us, while we was workin'. Then, unless he's took to the fields, he's a-goin' the same way we are. An' we're due to overhaul him. There'll only just be one of him; and there's two of us. I ain't aimin' to lose my slice of that two thousand; without hittin' a single lick to get it. If he—*sufferin' pink snakes!*"

In his sudden dismay, he drove down both feet on the pedals. The indignant car stalled. Through the blackness ahead, the white ray from the lamps had picked up a weird object. And the two brethren stared at it, slack-jawed.

Walking sedately on, in front of the stalled runabout, and in the exact centre of the dusty road, moved an animal. Huge and formless it bulked, as it receded into the fainter glow of light. It might have been anything from a lion to a bear; in that uncertain glimmer. But, the lamps' rays played strongly enough on one detail of the apparition to identify it, past doubt, to both the dumfounded onlookers. They saw, clearly enough, a white bundle suspended from the monster's jaws;—unquestionably the bundle which had been laid behind the alder.

For perhaps ten seconds the men sat moveless, gaping goggle-eyed. Then, the driver murmured in a faraway voice:

"Did you—did you—was you fool enough to think you seen anything? Was you, Eitel?"

"I-I sure seen *suthin'*, Roodie," quavered Eitel. "Suthin' with—with the kid in its mouth. It—"

"That's good enough for me!" announced the heroic Roodie, stamping again on the self-starter.

"If we both seen it, then it was *there*. And I'm goin' after it."

In another brace of seconds the lights once, more picked up the dark animal with its white bundle. Eitel shrank back in his seat. But Roodie put on another notch of gas. And, coming closer, both recognized the strange bundle-carrier as a dark-hued collie dog.

The identification did little to ease their feeling of incredulous mystification. But it banished their superstitious dread. Both of them were used to dogs. And though neither could guess how this particular dog happened to be stealing the twice-stolen baby, yet neither had the remotest fear of tackling the beast and rescuing its human plunder.

Roodie brought the abused runabout to another jerky stop within a few inches of the unconcerned collie. And he and Eitel swarmed earthward from opposite sides of the machine. In a trice, Roodie had struck Lad over the head; while Eitel grabbed at the bundle to drag it away from the dog.

Now, the weight of years was beginning to tell on Laddie. But that weight had not robbed him of the ability to call, at will, upon much of his oldtime strength and bewildering swiftness. Nor had it in any way dampened his hero-spirit or dulled his uncannily wise brain.

He had been plodding peacefully along, bearing home a wonderful gift—a gift oftener confided to the care of storks than of collies—when he had been attacked from two sides in most unprovoked fashion. He had been struck! His blood surged hot.

There was no Law governing such a case. So, as usual in new crises, Lad proceeded to make his own Law and to put it into effect.

A deft turn of the head eluded Eitel's snatching hand. With the lightness of a feather, Lad deposited the bundle in the soft dust of the road. In practically, the same gesture, the dog's curving eye-tooth slashed Eitel's outstretched wrist to the bone.

Then, staggering under a second head-blow from Roodie, the collie wheeled with lightning-swift fury upon this more hostile of his two assailants.

Hurling himself at the man's throat, in silent ferocity, he well-nigh turned the nocturnal battle into a killing. But Roodie's left arm, by instinct, flew up to guard his threatened jugular.

Through coat and shirt and skin and flesh,—as in the case of Lady's slayer,—the great dog's teeth clove their way; their rending snap checked only by the bone of the forearm. The impetus of his eighty-pound body sent the man clean off his balance. And together the two crashed backward to the ground.

Lad was not of the bulldog breed which seeks and gains a hold and then hangs on to it with locked jaws. A collie fights with brain as much as with teeth. By the time he and Roodie struck the earth, Lad tore free from the unloving embrace and whizzed about to face the second of his foes.

Eitel had taken advantage of the moment's respite to seize with his uninjured hand his slashed wrist. Then, on second thought, he released the wounded wrist and bent over the baby; with a view to picking him up and regaining the comparative safety of the car's floor. But his well-devised maneuver was not carried out.

For, as he leaned over the bundle, extending his hands to pick it up, Lad's teeth drove fiercely into the section of Eitel's plump anatomy which chanced to be presented to him by the stooping down of the kidnaper. Deep clove his sharp fangs. Nor did Eitel Schwartz sit down again with any degree of comfort for many a long day.

With resounding howls of pain, Eitel thrashed up and down the road; endeavoring to shake off this rear attack. The noise awakened the baby; who added his wails to the din. Roodie got dizzily to his feet; his left forearm useless and anguished from the tearing of its muscles:

"Shut up!" he bellowed. "You want to bring the whole county down on us? We—"

He ceased speaking; and lurched at full speed to the car and to the top of its single seat. For, at sound of his voice, Lad had loosed his grip on the screeching Eitel and whirled about on this earlier adversary.

The man reached the car-seat and slammed the door behind him, perhaps a sixth of a second too soon for Lad to reach him.

Eitel, warned by his brother's bawled command, made a rush for the other side of the machine and clambered up. He was a trifle less fortunate than had been Roodie, in making this ascent. For Lad's flashing jaws grazed his ankle and carried away in that snap a sample of Eitel's best town-going trousers.

Thus, on the seat of the car, swaying, and clutching at each other, crouched the two sore-wounded brethren; while Lad ravened about the vehicle, springing upward now and, again in futile effort to clear the top of the closed door.

Far down the road shone the lights of an approaching motor. Eitel dropped into the driving seat and set the runabout into motion. Once more, the dread of pursuit and of capture and of prison danced hideously before his frightened mental vision.

Barely missing the crying baby, as the runabout jerked forward, he made a fruitless attempt to run down the raging collie. Then he addressed himself to the business of getting himself and his brother as far out of the way as possible, before the oncoming car should reach the scene of strife.

As a matter of fact, the other car never reached this spot. Its occupants were two youths and two damsels, in search of a sequestered space of road where they might halt for a brief but delectable "petting party," on their way to a dance in the village. They found such a space, about a furlong on the thither side of the curve where the runabout had stopped. And they advanced no farther.

Lad, for a few rods, gave chase to the retreating Schwartzes. Then, the heavy exertions of the past minute or two began to exact toll on his aging body. Also, the baby was still whimpering in a drowsy monotone, as the paregoric sought to renew its sway on the racket awakened brain.

The dog turned pantingly back to the bundle; pawed it softly, as though to make sure the contents were not harmed; then once more picked it up gingerly between his reddened jaws; and continued his sedate homeward journey.

The Mistress and the Master were sitting on the veranda. It was almost bedtime. The Master arose, to begin his nightly task of locking the lower windows. From somewhere on the highroad that lay two hundred yards distant from the house, came the confused noise of shouts. Then, as he listened, the far-off sounds ceased. He went on with his task of locking up; and returned in a minute or two to the veranda.

As he did so, Lad came walking slowly up the porch steps. In his mouth he carried something large and white and dusty. This he proceeded to deposit with much care at the feet of the Mistress. Then he stood back; tail waving, dark eyes mischievously expectant.

"Another dividend from the curve!" laughed the Master. "What is it, this time? A pillow or—?"

He broke off in the middle of his amused query. For, even as he turned his flashlight on the dusty and blood-streaked bundle, the baby began once more to cry.

The local chief of police, in the village across the lake, was making ready for bed, when a telephone summons brought him back to his lower hallway.

"Hello!" came the Master's hail, over the wire. "Chief, has there been any alarm sent out for—for a missing baby?"

"Baby?" echoed the Chief. "No. Have you lost one?"

"No. I've found one. At least, Laddie has. He's just brought it home. It is dressed in unusually costly things, my wife says. There was a white baby-blanket strapped around it. And there are dust and streaks of fresh blood on the blanket. But the baby himself isn't hurt at all. And—"

"I'll be over there, in fifteen minutes," said the Chief, alive with professional interest.

But in ten minutes he was on the wire once more.

"Has the baby blanket got the monogram, 'B.R.R', on one corner?" he asked excitedly.

"Yes," answered the Master. "I was going to tell you that, when you hung up. And on—"

"That's the one!" fairly shouted the Chief. "As soon as you finished talking to me, I got another call. General alarm out for a kidnaped baby. Belongs to those Rennick people, up the Valley. The artists that rented the old Beasley place this summer. The baby was stolen, an hour ago; right out of the nursery. I'll phone 'em that he's found; and then I'll be over."

"All right. There's another queer point about all this. Our dog—"

"Speaking of dogs," went on the garrulous Chief, "this is a wakeful evening for me. I just got a call from the drug store that a couple of fellows have stopped there to get patched up from dog-bites. They say a dozen stray curs set on 'em, while they were changing a tire. The druggist thought they acted queer, contradicting each other in bits of their story. So he's taking his time, fixing them; till I can drop in on my way to your house and give 'em the once over. So—-"

"Do more than that!" decreed the Master, on quick inspiration.

"What I started to tell you is that there's blood on Lad's jaws; as well as on the baby's blanket. If two men say they've been bitten by dogs—"

"I get you!" yelled the other. "Good-by! I got no time to waste, when a clew like that is shaken in front of me. See you later!"

Long before the Chief arrived at the Place with triumphant tidings of his success in "sweating" the truth from the mangled and nerve-racked Schwartzes, the two other actors in the evening's drama were miles away among the sunflecked shadows of Dreamland.

The baby, industriously and unsanitarily sucking one pudgy thumb, was cuddled down to sleep in the Mistress's lap. And, in the depths of his cave under the living-room piano, Lad was stretched at perfect ease; his tiny white forepaws straight in front of him.

But his deep breathing was interrupted, now and then, by a muttered sigh. For, at last, one of his beautiful presents had failed to cause happiness and praise from his gods. Instead, it had apparently turned the whole household inside out; to judge by the noisy excitement and the telephoning and all. And, even in sleep, the old dog felt justly chagrined at the way his loveliest present to the Mistress had been received.

It was so hard to find out what humans would enjoy and what they wouldn't!

CHAPTER X.

THE INTRUDERS

It began with a gap in a line fence. The gap should never have been there. For, on the far side of it roamed creatures whose chief zest in life is the finding of such gaps and in breaking through for forage.

The Place's acreage ended, to northward, in the center of an oak grove whose northern half was owned by one Titus Romaine; a crabbed little farmer of the old school. Into his half of the grove, in autumn when mast lay thick and rich amid the tawny dead leaves, Romaine was wont to turn his herd of swine.

To Lad, the giant collie, this was always a trying season. For longer than he could remember, Lad had been the official watchdog of the Place. And his chief duties were to keep two-footed and four-footed strays from trespassing thereon.

To an inch, he knew the boundaries of the Master's land. And he knew that no human intruder was to be molested; so long as such intruder had the sense to walk straight down the driveway to the house. But woe to the tramp or other trespasser who chanced to come cross lots or to wander in any way off the drive! Woe also to such occasional cattle or other livestock as drifted in from the road or by way of a casual fence-gap!

Human invaders were to be met in drastic fashion. Quadruped trespassers were to be rounded up and swept at a gallop up the drive and out into the highroad. With cattle or with stray horses this was an easy job; and it contained, withal, much fun;—at least, for Lad.

But, pigs were different.

Experience and instinct had taught Lad what few humans realize. Namely, that of all created beasts, the pig is the worst and meanest and most vicious; and hardest to drive. When a horse or a cow, or a drove of them, wandered into the confines of the

Place, it was simple and joyous to head them off, turn them, set them into a gallop and send them on their journey at top speed. It took little skill and less trouble to do this. Besides, it was gorgeous sport. But pigs—!

When a porker wriggled and hunched and nosed a space in the line fence, and slithered greasily through, Lad's work was cut out for him. It looked simple enough. But it was not simple. Nor was it safe.

In the first instance, pigs were hard to start running. Oftener than not they would stand, braced, and glare at the oncoming collie from out their evil little red-rimmed eyes; the snouts above the hideous masked tushes quivering avidly. That meant Lad must circle them, at whirlwind speed; barking a thunderous fanfare to confuse them; and watching his chance to flash in and nip ear or flank; or otherwise get the brutes to running.

And, even on the run, they had an ugly way of wheeling, at close quarters, to face the pursuer. The razor tushes and the pronged forefeet were always ready, at such times, to wreak death on the dog, unless he should have the wit and the skill and the speed to change, in a breath, the direction of his dash. No, pigs were not pleasant trespassers. There was no fun in routing them. And there was real danger.

Except by dint of swiftness and of brain; an eighty-pound collie has no chance against a six-hundred-pound pig. The pig's hide, for one thing, is too thick to pierce with an average slash or nip: And the pig is too close to earth and too well-balanced by build and weight, to be overturned: And the tushes and forefeet can move with deceptive quickness. Also, back of the red-rimmed little eyes flickers the redder spirit of murder.

Locomotive engineers say a cow on a track is far less perilous to an oncoming train than is a pig. The former can be lifted, by the impact, and flung to one side. A pig, oftener than not, derails the engine. Standing with the bulk of its weight close to the ground, it is well-nigh as bad an obstacle to trains as would be a boulder of the same size. Lad had never met any engineers. But he had identically their opinion of pigs.

In all his long life, the great collie had never known fear. At least, he never had yielded to it. Wherefore, in the autumns, he had attacked with gay zest such of Titus Romaine's swine as had found their way through the fence.

But, nowadays, there was little enough of gay zest about anything Laddie did. For he was old;—very, very old. He had passed the fourteenth milestone. In other words, he was as old for a dog as is an octogenarian for a man.

Almost imperceptibly, but to his indignant annoyance, age had crept upon the big dog; gradually blurring his long clean lines; silvering his muzzle and eyebrows; flecking his burnished mahogany coat with stipples of silver; spreading to greater size the absurdly small white forepaws which were his one gross vanity; dulling a little the preternaturally keen hearing and narrowing the vision.

Yes, Lad was old. And he was a bit unwieldy from weight and from age. No longer could he lead Wolf and Bruce in the forest rabbit chases. Wherefore he stayed at home, for the most part and seldom strayed far from the Mistress and the Master whom he worshiped.

Moreover, he deputed the bulk of trespass-repelling to his fiery little son, Wolf; and to the graver and sweeter Bruce;—"Bruce, the Beautiful."

Which brings us by needfully prosy degrees to a morning, when two marauders came to the Place at the same time, if by different routes. They could not well have come at a more propitious time, for themselves; nor at a worse time for those whose domain they visited.

Bruce and Wolf had trotted idly off to the forest, back of the Place, for a desultory ramble in quest of rabbits or squirrels. This they had done because they were bored. For, the Mistress and the Master had driven over for the morning mail; and Lad had gone with them, as usual. Had it been night, instead of morning, neither

Wolf nor Bruce would have stirred a step from the grounds. For both were trained watchdogs, But, thus early in the day, neither duty nor companionship held them at home. And the autumn woods promised a half-hour of mild sport.

The superintendent and his helpers were in the distant "upper field," working around the roots of some young fruit trees. But for the maids, busy indoors, the Place was deserted of human or canine life.

Thus, luck was with the two intruders.

Through the fence-gap in the oak-grove, bored Titus Romaine's hugest and oldest and crankiest sow. She was in search of acorns and of any other food that might lie handy to her line of march. In her owner's part of the grove, there was too much competition, in the food-hunt, from other and equally greedy pigs of the herd. These she could fight off and drive from the choicest acorn-hoards. But it was easier to forage without competition.

So through the gap she forced her grunting bulk; and on through the Place's half of the oak-grove. Pausing now and then to root amid the strewn leaves, she made her leisurely way toward the open lawn with its two-hundred-year-old shade-oaks, and its flower-borders which still held a few toothsome bulbs.

The second intruder entered the grounds in much more open fashion. He was a man in the late twenties; well-set up, neatly, even sprucely, dressed; and he walked with a slight swagger. He looked very much at home and very certain of his welcome.

A casual student of human nature would have guessed him to be a traveling salesman, finely equipped with nerve and with confidence in his own goods. The average servant would have been vastly impressed with his air of self assurance; and would have admitted him to the house, without question. (The long-memoried warden of Auburn Prison would have recognized him as Alf Dugan, one of the cleverest automobile thieves in the East.)

Mr. Dugan was an industrious young man; as well as ingenious. And he had a streak of quick-witted audacity which made him an ornament to his chosen profession. His method of work was simple. Coming to a rural neighborhood, he would stop at some local hotel, and, armed with clever patter and a sheaf of automobile insurance documents, would make the rounds of the region's better-class homes.

At these he sold no automobile insurance; though he made seemingly earnest efforts to do so. But he learned the precise location of each garage; the cars therein; and the easiest way to the highroad, and any possible obstacles to a hasty flight thereto. Usually, he succeeded in persuading his reluctant host to take him to the garage to look at the cars and to estimate the insurable value of each. While there, it was easy to palm a key or to get a good look at the garage padlock for future skeleton-key reference; or to note what sort of car-locks were used.

A night or two later, the garage was entered and the best car was stolen. Dugan, like love, laughed at locksmiths.

Sometimes,—notably in places where dogs were kept,—he would make his initial visit and then, choosing a time when he had seen some of the house's occupants go for a walk with their dogs, would enter by broad daylight, and take a chance at getting the car out, unobserved. If he were interrupted before starting off in the machine, why, he was that same polite insurance aunt who had come back to revise his estimate on the premium needed for the car; and was taking another look at it to make certain. Once in the driver's seat and with the engine going, he had no fear of capture. A whizzing rush to the highroad and down it to the point where his confederate waited with the new number-plates; and he could snap his fat fingers at pursuit.

Dugan had called at the Place, a week earlier. He had taken interested note of the little garage's two cars and of the unlocked garage doors. He had taken less approving note of the three guardian collies: Lad, still magnificent and formidable, in spite of his weight of years;—Bruce, gloriously beautiful and stately and aloof;—young Wolf, with the fire and fierce agility of a tiger-cat. All three had watched him, grimly. None had offered the slightest move to make friends with the smooth-spoken visitor. Dogs have a queerly occult sixth sense, sometimes, in regard to those who mean ill to their masters.

This morning, idling along the highroad, a furlong from the Place's stone gateway, Dugan had seen the Mistress and the Master drive past in the smaller of the two cars. He had seen Lad with them. A little later, he had seen the men cross the road toward the upper field. Then, almost on the men's heels, he had seen Bruce and Wolf canter across the same road; headed for the forest. And Dugan's correctly stolid face rippled into a pleased smile.

Quickening his pace, he hurried on to the gateway and down the drive. But, as he passed the house on his way to the garage where stood the other and larger car, he paused. Out of an ever-vigilant eye-corner, he saw an automobile turn in at the gateway, two hundred yards up the wooded slope; and start down the drive.

The Mistress and the Master were returning from the post office.

Dugan's smile vanished. He stopped in his tracks; and did some fast thinking. Then, mounting the veranda steps, he knocked boldly at a side door; the door nearest to him. As the maids were in the kitchen or making up the bedrooms, his knock was unheard. Half hidden by the veranda vines, he waited.

The car came down the driveway and circled the house to the side farthest from Dugan. There, at the front door, it halted. The Mistress and Lad got out. The Master did not go down to the garage. Instead, he circled the house again; and chugged off up the drive; bound for the station to meet a guest whose train was due in another ten minutes. Dugan drew a long breath; and swaggered toward the garage. His walk and manner had in them an easy openness that no honest man's could possibly have acquired in a lifetime.

The Mistress, deposited at the front veranda, chirped to Lad; and started across the lawn toward the chrysanthemum bed, a hundred feet away.

The summer's flowers were gone—even to the latest thin stemmed

Teplitz rose and the last stalk of rose-tinted cosmos. For dining table, now, and for living-room and guest rooms, nothing was left but the mauve and bronze hardy chrysanthemums which made gay the flower border at the crest of the lawn overlooking the lake. Thither fared the Mistress, in search of blossoms.

Between her and the chrysanthemum border was a bed of canvas. Frost had smitten the tall, dark stems; leaving only a copse of brown stalks. Out of this copse, chewing greedily at an uprooted bunch of canna-bulbs, slouched Romaine's wandering sow. At, sight of the Mistress, she paused in her leisurely progress and, with the bunch of bulbs still hanging from one corner of her shark-mouth, stood blinking truculently at the astonished woman.

Now, Lad had not obeyed the Mistress's soft chirp. It had not reached his dulling ears;—the ears which, of old, had caught her faintest whisper. Yet, he would have followed her, as ever, without such summons, had not his nostrils suddenly become aware of an alien scent.

Lad's sense of smell, like his hearing, was far less keen than once it had been. But, it was still strong enough to register the trace of intruders. His hackles bristled. Up went the classically splendid head, to sniff the light breeze, for further information as to the reek of pig and the lighter but more disquieting scent of man.

Turning his head, to reinforce with his near-sighted eyes the failing evidence of his nostrils, he saw the sow emerge from the canna-clump. He saw, too—or he divined—the look in her pale little red-rimmed eyes; as they glared defiantly at the Mistress. And Lad cleared the porch steps at one long leap.

For the instant, he forgot he was aged and stout and that his joints ached at any sudden motion; and that his wind and his heart were not what they had been;—and that his once-terrible fangs were yellowed and blunt; and that his primal strength was forever fled. Peril was facing the Mistress. That was all Laddie knew or cared. With his wonted trumpet-bark of challenge, he sped toward her.

The Mistress, recovering from her surprise at the apparition of the huge pig, noticed the bunch of canna-bulbs dangling from the slobbery lips. This very week all the bulbs were to have been dug up and taken into the greenhouse, for the winter. Angered,—with all a true flower-lover's indignation,—at this desecrating of one of her beloved plants, she caught up a stick which had been used as a rose-prop. Brandishing this, and crying "Shoo!" very valiantly indeed, she advanced upon the sow.

The latter did not stir; except to lower her bristling head an inch or so; and let drop the bunch of bulbs from between her razor-teeth. The Mistress advanced another step; and struck at the beast.

The sow veered, to avoid the blow; then, with ludicrous yet deadly swiftness, wheeled back and charged straight for the woman.

Many a child and not a few grown men and women have gone down under such murderous charges; to be trampled and gouged and torn to death, before help could come. But the slaveringly foul jaws did not so much as touch the hem of the Mistress's dress.

Between her and the sow flashed a swirl of mahogany-and-snow. Lad, charging at full speed, crashed into the forward-lurching six-hundredweight of solid flesh and inch-thick hide.

The impact bowled him clean over, knocking the breath out of him. Not from choice had he made such a blundering and un-collielike attack. In other days, he could have flashed in and out again, with the speed of light; leaving his antagonist with a slashed face or even a broken leg, as souvenir of his assault. But those days were past. His uncannily wise brain and his dauntless courage were all that remained of his ancient prowess. And this brain and pluck told him his one chance of checking the sow's charge on the Mistress was to hurl himself full at her.

His impetus, which had knock him flat, scarce slowed down the pig's lurching rush; scarce enabled the frightened Mistress to recoil a step. Then, the sow was lunging at her again, over the prostrate dog's body.

But, even as he fell, Lad had gathered his feet under him. And the shock which knocked him breathless did not make the wise brain waver in its plan of campaign. Before he sought to rise, up drove his bared teeth, at the sow that was plunging across him. And those teeth clove deep into her pinkish nostrils;—well-nigh the only vulnerable spot, (as Lad knew) in her bristling pigskin armor.

Lad got his grip. And, with all his fragile old strength, he hung on; grinding the outworn fangs further and further into the sensitive nose of his squealing foe.

This stopped the sow's impetuous charge; for good and all. With a heavy collie hanging to one's tortured nose and that collie's teeth sunk deep into it, there is no scope for thinking of any other opponent. She halted, striking furiously, with her sharp cloven fore-hoofs, at the writhing dog beneath her.

One ferociously driving hoof cut a gash in Lad's chest. Another tore the skin from his shoulder. Unheeding, he hung on. The sow braced herself, solid, on outspread legs; and shook her head and forequarters with all her muscular might.

Lad was hurled free, his weakened jaws failing to withstand such a yank. Over and over he rolled, to one side; the sow charging after him. She had lost all interest in attacking the Mistress. Her flaming little brain now held no thought except to kill and mangle the dog that had hurt her snout so cruelly. And she rushed at him, the tushes glinting from under her upcurled and bleeding lips.

But, the collie, for all his years and unwieldiness, was still a collie. And, by the time he stopped rolling, he was scrambling to his feet. Shrinking quickly to one side, as the sow bore down upon him, he eluded her rush, by the fraction of an inch; and made a wolflike slash for her underbody, as she hurtled by.

The blunted eyetooth made but a superficial furrow; which served only to madden its victim still further. Wheeling, she returned to the attack. Again, with a ghost of his old elusive speed; Laddie avoided her rush, by the narrowest of margins; and, snapping furiously, caught her by the ear.

Now, more than once, in other frays, Lad had subdued and scared trespassing pigs by this hold. But, in those days, his teeth had been keen and his jaw strong enough to crack a beef bone. Moreover, the pigs on which he had used it to such effect were not drunk with the lust of killing.

The sow squealed, afresh, with pain; and once more braced herself and shook her head with all her might: Again, Lad was flung aside by that shake; this time with a fragment of torn ear between his teeth.

As she drove slaveringly at him once more, Lad swerved and darted in; diving for her forelegs. With the collie, as with his ancestor, the wolf, this dive for the leg of an enemy is a favorite and tremendously effective trick in battle. Lad found his hold, just above the right pastern. And he exerted every atom of his power to break the bone or to sever the tendon.

In all the Bible's myriad tragic lines there is perhaps none other so infinitely sad,—less for its actual significance than for what it implies to every man or woman or animal, soon or late,—than that which describes the shorn Samson going forth in jaunty confidence to meet the Philistines he so often and so easily had conquered:

"He wist not that the Lord was departed from him!"

To all of us, to whom the doubtful blessing of old age is granted, must come the black time when we shall essay a task which once we could accomplish with ease;—only to find its achievement has passed forever beyond our waning powers. And so, this day, was it with Sunnybank Lad.

Of yore, such a grip as he now secured would have ham strung or otherwise maimed its victim and left her wallowing helpless. But the dull teeth merely barked the leg's tough skin. And a spasmodic jerk ripped it loose from the dog's hold.

Lad barely had time to spring aside, to dodge the wheeling sow. He was panting heavily. His wounds were hurting and weakening him. His wind was gone. His heart was doing queer things which made him sick and dizzy. His strength was turning to water. His courage alone blazed high and undimmed.

Not once did it occur to him to seek safety in flight. He must have known the probable outcome. For Lad knew much. But the great heart did not flinch at the prospect. Feebly, yet dauntlessly, he came back to the hopeless battle. The Mistress was in danger. And he alone could help.

No longer able to avoid the rushes, he met some of them with pathetically useless jaws; going down under others and rising with ever greater slowness and difficulty. The sow's ravening teeth found a goal, more than once, in the burnished mahogany coat which the Mistress brushed every day with such loving care. The pronged hoofs had twice more cut him as he strove to roll aside from their onslaught after one of his heavy tumbles.

The end of the fight seemed very near. Yet Lad fought on. To the attack, after each upset or wound, he crawled with deathless courage.

The Mistress, at Lad's first charge, had stepped back. But, at once she had caught up again the stick and belabored the sow with all her frail muscular might. She might as well have been beating the side of a concrete wall. Heedless of the flailing, the sow ignored her; and continued her maddened assault on Lad. The maids, attracted by the noise, crowded the front doorway; clinging together and jabbering. To them the Mistress called now for the Master's shotgun, from the study wall, and for a handful of shells.

She kept her head; though she saw she was powerless to save the dog she loved. And her soul was sick within her at his peril which her puny efforts could not avert.

Running across the lawn, toward the house, she met half way the maid who came trembling forth with the gun and two shells. Without stopping to glance at the cartridges,—nor to realize that they were filled with Number Eight shot, for quails,—she thrust two of them into the breech and, turning, fired pointblank at the sow.

Lad was down again; and the sow,—no longer in a squealing rush, but with a new cold deadliness,—was gauging the distance to his exposed throat. The first shot peppered her shoulder; the tiny pellets scarce scratching the tough hide.

The Mistress had, halted, to fire. Now, she ran forward: With the muzzle not three feet from the sow's head, she pulled trigger again.

The pig's huge jaws road opened with deliberate width. One forefoot was pinning the helplessly battling dog to earth, while she made ready to tear out his throat.

The second shot whizzed about her head and face. Two or three of the pellets entered the open mouth.

With a sound that was neither grunt nor howl, yet which savored of both, the sow lurched back from the flash and roar and the anguishing pain in her tender mouth. The Mistress whirled aloft the empty and useless gun and brought it crashing down on the pig's skull. The carved mahogany stock broke in two. The jar of impact knocked the weapon from its wielder's numbed fingers.

The sow seemed scarce to notice the blow. She continued backing away; and champed her jaws as if to locate the cause of the agony in her mouth. Her eyes were inflamed and dazed by the flash of the gun.

The Mistress took advantage of the moment's breathing space to bend over the staggeringly rising Lad; and, catching him by the ruff, to urge him toward the house. For once, the big collie refused to obey. He knew pig nature better than did she. And he knew the sow was not yet finished with the battle. He strove to break free from the loved grasp and to stagger back to his adversary.

The Mistress, by main strength, drew him, snarling and protesting, toward the safety of the house. Panting, bleeding, reeling, pitiably weak, yet he resisted the tender urging; and kept twisting his bloody head back for a glimpse of his foe. Nor was the precaution useless. For, before the Mistress and her wounded dog were half-way across the remaining strip of lawn, the sow recovered enough of her deflected wits and fury to lower her head and gallop down after them.

At her first step, Lad, by a stupendous effort, wrenched free from the Mistress's clasp; and flung himself between her and the charging mass of pork. But, as he did so, he found breath for a trumpet-bark that sounded more like a rallying cry.

For, dulled as were his ears, they were still keener than any human's. And they had caught the sound of eight flying paws amid the dead leaves of the drive. Wolf and Bruce, coming home at a leisurely trot, from their ramble in the forest, had heard the two reports of the shotgun; and had broken into a run. They read the meaning in Lad's exhausted bark, as clearly as humans might read a printed word. And it lent wings to their feet.

Around the corner of the house tore the two returning collies. In a single glance, they seemed to take in the whole grisly scene. They, too, had had their bouts with marauding swine; and they were still young enough to enjoy such clashes and to partake of them without danger.

The sow, too blind with pain and rage to know reinforcements were coming to the aid of the half-dead hero, tore forward. The Mistress, with both hands, sought to drag Lad behind her. The maids screeched in plangent chorus.

Then, just as the sow was launching herself on the futilely snapping Lad, she was stupidly aware that the dog had somehow changed to three dogs. One of these three the Mistress was still holding. The two others, with excellent teamwork, were assailing the sow from opposite sides.

She came to a sliding stop in her charge; blinking in bewildered fury.

Bruce had caught her by the torn left ear; and was keeping easily out of her way, while he inflicted torture thereon. Wolf, like a furry whirlwind, had stopped only long enough to slash her bleeding nose to the bone; and now was tearing away at her hind leg in an industrious and very promising effort to hamstring her. In front, Lad was still straining to break the Mistress's loving hold; and to get at his pestered enemy.

This was more than the huge porker had bargained for. Through all her murder-rage, she had sense enough to know she was outnumbered and beaten. She broke into a clumsy gallop; heading homeward.

But Bruce and Wolf would not have it so. Delightedly they tore in to the attack. Their slashing fangs and their keenly nipping front teeth were everywhere. They were all over her. In sudden panic, blinded by terror and pain, the sow put her six hundred pounds of unwieldy weight into the fastest motion she could summon. At a scrambling run, she set off, around the house; head down, bitten tail aloft; the two dogs at her bleeding haunches.

Dimly, she saw a big and black obstacle loom up in her path. It was coming noisily toward her. But she was going too fast and too blindly to swerve. And she met it, headlong; throwing her vast weight forward in an attempt to smash through it. At the same time, Wolf and Bruce left off harrying her flanks and sprang aside.

Dugan had reached the garage unseen. There, he had backed out the car, by hand; shoving it into the open, lest the motor-whirr give premature announcement of his presence. Then, as he boarded the machine and reached for the self-starter, all bedlam broke loose, from somewhere in the general direction of the house, fifty yards away.

Dugan, glancing up apprehensively, beheld the first phases of the fight. Forgetting the need of haste and of secrecy, he sat there, open-mouthed, watching a scrimmage which was beyond all his sporting experience and which thrilled him as no prize-fight had ever done. Moveless, wide eyed, he witnessed the battle.

But the arrival of the two other dogs and the flight of the sow roused him to a sense of the business which had brought him thither. The Mistress and the maids had no eyes or ears for anything but the wounded Lad. Dugan knew he could, in all probability, drive to the main road unnoticed; if he should keep the house between him and the women.

He pressed the self-starter; threw off the brake and put the car into motion. Then, as he struck the level stretch of driveway, back of the house, he stepped hard on the accelerator. Here, for a few rods, was danger of recognition; and it behooved him to make speed. He made it.

Forward bounded the car and struck a forty-mile gait. And around the house's far corner and straight toward Dugan came flying the sow and the two collies. The dogs, at sight of the onrushing car, sprang aside. The sow did not.

In the narrow roadway there was no room for Dugan to turn out. Nor did he care to. Again and again he had run over dogs, without harming his car or slackening its pace. And of course it would be the same with a pig. He stepped harder on the accelerator.

Alf Dugan came to his senses in the hospital ward of the Paterson jail. He had not the faintest idea how he chanced to be there. When they told him the car had turned turtle and that he and a broken-necked pig had been hauled out of the wreckage, he asked in all honesty:

"What car? What pig? Quit stringing me, can't you? Which of my legs did you say is bust, and which one is just twisted? They both feel as bad as each other. How'd I get here, anyhow? What happened me?"

When the vet had worked over Lad for an hour and had patched him up and had declared there was no doubt at all about his getting well, Wolf and Bruce were brought in to see the invalid. The Mistress thought he might be glad to see them.

He was not.

Indeed, after one scornful look in their direction, Laddie turned away from the visitors, in cold disgust. Also, he was less demonstrative with the Mistress, than usual. Anyone could see his feelings were deeply hurt. And anyone who knew Lad could tell why.

He had borne the brunt of the fight. And, at the last, these lesser dogs had won the victory without his aid. Still worse, his beloved Mistress,—for whom he had so blithely staked his aged life,—the Mistress had held him back by force from joining in the delirious last phases of the battle. She had made him stand tamely by, while others finished the grand work he had begun.

It was not fair. And Laddie let everyone in sight know it was not fair; and that he had no intention of being petted into a good humor.

Still, when, by and by, the Mistress sat down on the floor beside him and told him what a darling and wonderful and heroic dog he was and how proud she felt of his courage, and when her dear hand rumpled the soft hair behind his ears,—well, somehow Lad found himself laying his head in her lap; and making croony low sounds at her and pretending to bite her little white hand.

It was always hard to stay offended at the Mistress.

CHAPTER XI.

THE GUARD

Lad was old—very, very old. He had passed his sixteenth birthday. For a collie, sixteen is as old as is ninety-five for a human.

The great dog's life had been as beautiful as himself. And now, in the late twilight of his years, Time's hand rested on him as lovingly as did the Mistress's. He had few of the distressing features of age.

True; his hearing was duller than of yore. The magnificent body's lines were blurred with flesh. The classic muzzle was snow white; as were the lashes and eyebrows. And the once mighty muscles were stiff and unwieldy. Increasing feebleness crept over him, making exercise a burden and any sudden motion a pain. The once trumpeting bark was a hollow echo of itself.

But the deep-set dark eyes, with a soul looking out of them, were as clear as ever. The uncannily wise brain had lost not an atom of its power. The glorious mahogany-and-snow coat was still abundant. The fearlessly gay spirit and loyal heart were undimmed by age.

Laddie resented angrily his new limitations. From time to time he would forget them; and would set off at a run in the wake of Bruce and Wolf, when the sound of a stranger's approach made them gallop up the driveway to investigate. But always; after the first few stiff bounds, he would come to a panting halt and turn back wearily to his resting place in the veranda's coolest corner; as indignant over his own weakness, as he would have been at fetters which impeded his limbs.

He was more and more sensitive about this awkward feebleness of his. And he sought to mask it; in ways that seemed infinitely pathetic to the two humans who loved him. For instance, one of his favorite romps in bygone days had been to throw himself down in front of the Mistress and pretend to bite her little feet; growling terrifically as he did it. Twice of late, as he had been walking at her side, his footing had slipped or he had lost his balance, and had tumbled headlong Instantly, both times, he had begun to growl and had bitten in mock fury at the Mistress's foot. By this pitiful ruse he strove to make her believe that his fall had been purposeful and a part of the olden game.

But worst of all he missed the long walks on which, from puppyhood, he had always accompanied the Mistress and the Master. Unknown to the old dog, these walks had been shortened, mercifully, and slowed down, to accommodate themselves to Lad's waning strength: But the time came when even a half-mile, at snail-pace, over a smooth road, was too much for his wind and endurance.

Nowadays, when they were going for a walk, Lad was first lured into the house and left there. The ruse did not fool him, any more than it would have deceived a grown man. And his feelings were cruelly hurt at every instance of this seeming defection on the part of his two worshiped human chums.

"He still enjoys life," mused the Master, one day in late summer, as he and the Mistress sat on the veranda, with Lad asleep at their feet. "And he can still get about a bit. His appetite is good, and he drowses happily for a good deal of the day; and the car-rides are still as much fun for him as ever they were. But when the time comes—and he's breaking fast, these past few months—when the time comes that life is a misery to him—"

"I know," interposed the Mistress, her voice not quite steady. "I know. Do you suppose I haven't been thinking about it, on the hot nights when I couldn't sleep? But, when the time comes—when it comes—you'll—you'll do it, yourself, won't you?"

"Yes," promised the Master, miserably. "No one else shall. I'd rather cut off one of my own hands, though. *I've* been doing a bit of thinking, too—at night. It's nobody's job but mine. Laddie would rather have it that way, I know. And, by a bullet. He's a gallant old soldier. And that is the way for him to go. Now, for the Lord's

sake, let's talk about something else! A man or woman is a fool to
care that way about any mere dog. I—"

"But Lad isn't a 'mere' dog," contradicted the Mistress, stooping
to pet the collie's classic head as it lay across her foot. "He's—he's
Laddie."

The sound of his name pierced the sleep mists and brought
the dog to wakefulness. He raised his head inquiringly toward
the Mistress, and his plumed tail began to thump the floor. The
Mistress patted him again; and spoke a word or two. Lad prepared
to drowse once more. Then, to his dulled ears came the padding
of little bare feet on the grass. And he glanced up again, this time
in eager interest.

Across the lawn from the orchard came trotting a child; carrying
a basket of peaches toward the kitchen. The youngster wore but
a single garment, a shapeless calico dress that fell scarcely to her
knees. She was Sonya, the seven-year-old daughter of one of the
Place's extra workmen, a Slav named Ruloff who lived in the mile-
distant village, across the lake.

Ruloff, following the custom of his peasant ancestors, put
his whole family to work, from the time its members were old
enough to toddle. And he urged them against the vice of laziness
by means of an ever-ready fist, or a still readier toe or a harness
strap—whichever of the trio of energy producers chanced to be
handiest. In coming over to the Place, for a month's labor, during
the harvest season, he brought along every day his youngest and
most fragile offspring, Sonya. Under her father's directions and
under his more drastic modes of encouragement, the little girl was
of much help to him in his doily toil.

Twice, the Master had caught him punishing her for undue
slowness in carrying out some duty too heavy for her frail strength.
On both times he had stopped the brutal treatment. On the second,
he had told Ruloff he would not only discharge him, but assist
his departure from the Place with a taste of boot-toe medicine,
if ever the Slav should lay a hand on the child again during his

period of employment there. The Place's English superintendent had promised like treatment to the man, should he catch him ill treating Sonya.

Wherefore, Ruloff had perforce curbed his parental urgings toward violence;—at least during the hours when he and the child were on the Place.

Sonya was an engaging little thing; and the Mistress had made a pet of her. So had the Master. But the youngster's warmest friend was old Sunnybank Lad.

From the first day of Sonya's advent in his life, Lad had constituted himself her adorer and constant companion.

Always his big heart had gone out to children; as to everything weak and defenseless. Not always had his treatment at the hands of children encouraged this feeling of loving chivalry and devotion. But Sonya was an exception. Whenever she could steal a minute of time, away from her father's glum eyes and nagging voice and ready fist, she would seek out Lad.

She was as gentle with the grand old dog as other children had been rough. She loved to cuddle down close beside him, her arms around his shaggy neck; and croon queer little high-voiced songs to him; her thin cheek against his head. She used to save out fragments from her own sparse lunch to give to him. She was inordinately proud to walk at his side during Lad's rare rambles around the Place. Child and dog made a pretty picture of utter chumship.

To nobody save the Mistress and the Master had Laddie ever given his heart so completely as to this baby.

Hurried though she was, today, Sonya set down her basket of peaches and, with a shy glance of appeal at the two humans, reached across the veranda edge to stroke Lad's head and to accept in delight his proffered paw. Then, guiltily, she caught up her basket and sped on to the kitchen.

Lad, slowly and with difficulty, got to his feet and followed her. A minute later the Mistress watched them making their way to the orchard, side by side; the child slackening her eager steps in order to keep pace with the aged dog.

"I wish we could arrange to take her away from that brute of a father of hers, and keep her here," said the Mistress. "It's horrible to think of such a helpless wisp of a baby being beaten and made to work, day and night. And then she and Laddie love each other so. They—"

"What can we do?" asked the Master, hopelessly. "I've spoken to the village authorities about it. But it seems the law can't interfere; unless brutal cruelty can be proved or unless the parents are unfit to bring up the child."

"Brutal cruelty?" echoed the Mistress. "What could be more brutal than the way he beats her? Why, last week there was a bruise on her arm as big—"

"What can we prove? He has a legal right to punish her. If we got them up in court, he'd frighten her into swearing she hurt her arm on a fence picket and that he never harms her. No, there's no sort of cure for the rotten state of affairs."

But the Master was mistaken. There was a very good cure indeed for it. And that cure was being applied at the moment he denied its existence.

Sonya had disappeared from view over the crest of the lawn: Down into the orchard she went, Lad at her side; to where Ruloff was waiting for her to lug another full basket back to the house.

"Move!" he ordered, as she drew near. "Don't crawl! Move, or I'll make you move."

This threat he voiced very bravely indeed. He was well out of sight of the house. The superintendent and the two other men were working on the far side of the hill. It seemed an eminently safe time to exercise his parental authority. And, hand uplifted, he took a threatening step toward the little girl.

Sonya cowered back in mortal dread. There was no mistaking the import of Ruloff's tone or gesture. Lad read it as clearly as did the child. As Sonya shrank away from the menace, a furry shoulder was pressed reassuringly against her side. Lad's cold muzzle was thrust for the merest instant into her trembling hand.

Then, as Ruloff advanced, Lad took one majestic step forward; his great body shielding the girl; his dark eyes sternly on the man's; his lips drawing back from his blunted yellow fangs. Deep in his throat a growl was born.

Ruloff checked himself; looking doubtfully at the shaggy brute. And at the same moment the superintendent appeared over the ridge of the hill, on his way to the orchard. The Slav picked up a filled basket and shoved it at Sonya.

"Jump!" he ordered. "Keep moving. Be back here in one minute!"

With a sigh of enormous relief and a pat of furtive gratitude to Lad, the child set forth on her errand. Yet, even at risk of a sharper rebuke, she accommodated her pace to Lad's stately slow steps.

Hitherto she had loved the dog for no special reason except that her heart somehow went out to him. But now she had a practical cause for her devotion. Lad had stood between her and a fist blow. He had risked, she knew not what, to defy her all-terrible father and to protect her from punishment.

As soon as she was out of Ruloff's sight, she set down her basket, and flung both puny arms about the dog's neck in an agony of gratitude.

Her squeeze almost strangled the weak old collie. But there was love in it. And because of that, he reveled in the hurt.

"You won't let him thump me!" she whispered in the dog's ear. "You won't let him. I'd never be afraid of him, if you were there. Oh, Laddie, you're so darling!"

Lad, highly pleased, licked her wizened little face and, sitting down, insisted on shaking hands with her. He realized he had done something quite wonderful and had made this little chum of his proud of him. Wherefore, he was proud of himself; and felt young and gay again;—until his next strenuous effort to walk fast.

All night, in her sleep, in the stiflingly hot loft of her father's hovel, which served her and the five other Ruloff children as a dormitory, Sonya was faintly aware of that bright memory. Her first waking thought was of the shaggy shoulder pressed so protectingly against her side; and of the reassuring thrust of Lad's muzzle into her cupped palm. It all seemed as vividly real as though she could still feel the friendly contact.

On the next morning, Ruloff alone of all the village's population went to work. For it was Labor Day.

Ruloff did not believe in holidays,—either for himself or for his family. And while wages were so high he was not minded to throw away a full day's earnings, just for the sake of honoring a holiday ordained in a country for which he felt no fondness or other interest. So, with Sonya tagging after him, he made his way to the Place, as usual.

Now, on Labor Day, of that year, was held the annual outdoor dog-show at Hawthorne. Lad, of course, was far too old to be taken to a show. And this was one of the compensations of old age. For Laddie detested dog shows. But, abnormally sensitive by nature, this sensitiveness had grown upon him with failing strength and added years. Thus, when he saw Bruce and Bob and Jean bathed and groomed and made ready for the show, he was sad at heart. For here was one more thing in which he no longer had any share.

And so he lay down in his cave, under the piano, his head between his absurdly small white forepaws; and hearkened sadly to the preparations for departure.

Bruce ("Sunnybank Goldsmith") was perhaps the most beautiful collie of his generation. Groomed for a show, he made most other dogs look plebeian and shabby. That day, one may say in passing, he was destined to go through the collie classes, to Winners, with a rush; and then to win the award and cup for "Best Dog Of Any Breed In The Show."

Bruce's son and daughter—Bobby and Jean were to win in their respective collie classes as Best Puppy and Best Novice. It was to be a day of triumph for the Sunnybank Kennels. Yet, somehow, it was to be a day to which the Mistress and the Master never enjoyed looking back.

Into the car the three dogs were put. The Mistress and the Master and the Place's superintended got aboard, and the trip to Hawthorne began.

Laddie had come out from his cave to see the show-goers off. The Mistress, looking back, had a last glimpse of him, standing in the front doorway; staring wistfully after the car. She waved her hand to him in farewell. Lad wagged his plumed tail, once, in reply, to the salute. Then, heavily, he turned back again into the house.

"Dear old Laddie!" sighed the Mistress. "He used to hate to go to shows. And now he hates being left behind. It seems so cruel to leave him. And yet—"

"Oh the maids will take good care of him!" consoled the Master. "They spoil him, whenever they get a chance. And we'll be back before five o'clock. We can't be forever looking out for his crotchety feelings."

"We won't be 'forever' doing that," prophesied the Mistress, unhappily.

Left alone the old dog paced slowly back to his cave. The day was hot. His massive coat was a burden. Life was growing more of a problem than of old it had been. Also, from time to time, lately, his heart did queer things that annoyed Lad. At some sudden motion or undue exertion it had a new way of throbbing and of hammering against his ribs so violently as to make him pant.

Lad did not understand this. And, as with most things he did not understand, it vexed him. This morning, for example,—the heat of the day and the fatigue of his ramble down through the rose garden to the lake and back, had set it to thumping painfully. He was glad to lie at peace in his beloved cave, in the cool music-room; and sleep away the hours until his deities should return from that miserable dog-show. He slept.

And so an hour wore on; and then another and another.

At the show, the Mistress developed one of her sick headaches.

She said nothing of it. But the Master saw the black shadows grow, under her eyes; and the color go out of her face; and he noted the little pain-lines around her mouth. So, as soon as the collie judging was over, he made her get into the car; and he drove her home, meaning to return to Hawthorne in time for the afternoon judging of specials and of variety classes.

Meanwhile, as the morning passed, Lad was roused from his fitful old-age slumber by the sound of crying. Into his dreams seeped the distressing sound. He woke; listened; got up painfully and started toward the front door.

Halfway to the door, his brain cleared sufficiently for him to recognize the voice that had awakened him. And his leisurely walk merged into a run.

Ruloff and Sonya had been working all morning in the peach orchard. To the child's chagrin, Lad was nowhere in sight. Every time she passed the house she loitered as long as she dared, in hope of getting a glimpse of him.

"I wonder where Laddie is," she ventured, once, as her father was filling a basket for her to carry.

"The dogs have gone to a silly show," grunted Ruloff, piling the basket. "The superintendent told me, yesterday. To waste a whole day with dogs! Pouf! No wonder the world is poor! Here, the basket is full. Jump!"

Sonya picked up the heavy load—twice as big as usual were the baskets given her to carry, now that the interfering Master and the superintendent were not here to forbid—and started laboriously for the house.

Her back ached with weariness. Yet, in the absence of her protectors, she dared not complain or even to allow herself the luxury of walking slowly. So, up the hill, she toiled; at top speed. Ruloff had finished filling another basket, and he prepared to follow her. This completed the morning's work. His lunch-pail awaited him at the barn. With nobody to keep tabs on him, he resolved to steal an extra hour of time, in honor of Labor Day—at his employer's expense.

Sonya pattered up the rise and around to the corner of the house. There, feeling her father's eye on her, as he followed; she tried to hasten her staggering steps. As a result, she stumbled against the concrete walk. Her bare feet went from under her.

Down she fell, asprawl; the peaches flying in fifty directions. She had cut her knee, painfully, against the concrete edge. This, and the knowledge that Ruloff would most assuredly punish her clumsiness, made her break out in shrill weeping.

Among the cascaded peaches she lay, crying her eyes out. Up the hill toward her scrambled Ruloff; basket on shoulder; yelling abuse better fitted for the ears of a balky mule than for those of a hurt child.

"Get up!" he bawled. "Get up, you worthless little cow! If you've spoiled any of those peaches or broke my basket, I'll cut the flesh off your bones."

Sonya redoubled her wailing. For, she recognized a bumpy substance beneath her as the crushed basket. And these baskets belonged to Ruloff; not to the Place.

For the accidental breaking of far less worthwhile things, at home, she and her brothers and sisters had often been thrashed most unmercifully: Her lamentations soared to high heaven. And her father's running feet sounded like the tramp of Doom.

There is perhaps no other terror so awful as that of an ill treated child at the approach of punishment. A man or woman, menaced by danger from law or from private foe, can either fight it out or run away from it. But there is no hiding place for a child from a brute parent. The punishment is as inevitable and as fearsome as from the hand of God.

No; there is no other terror so awful. And, one likes to think, there is no other punishment in the next world so severe as that meted out to the torturers of little children. For this hope's basis there is the solemn warning voiced by the All-pitying Friend of children;—a threat which, apparently, was unfamiliar to Ruloff.

Down upon the weepingly prostrate Sonya bore the man. As

he came toward her, he ripped off the leathern belt he wore. And he brandished it by the hole-punch end; the brass buckle singing ominously about his head. Then, out from the house and across the wide veranda flashed a giant tawny shape.

With the fierce speed of his youngest days, Lad cleared the porch and reached the crying child. In the same instant he beheld the advancing Ruloff; and the wise old brain read the situation at a glance.

Stopping only to lick the tear-streaked little face, Lad bounded in front of Sonya and faced the father. The collie's feeble old body was tense; his eyes blazed with indignant fury. His hackles bristled. The yellowed and useless teeth glinted from beneath back-writhed lips. For all his age, Lad was a terrible and terrifying figure as he stood guard over the helpless waif.

Ruloff hesitated an instant, taken aback by the apparition. Sonya ceased shrieking. Lad was here to protect her. Over her frightened soul came that former queer sense of safety. She got up, tremblingly, and pressed close to the furry giant who had come to her rescue. She glared defiantly up at Ruloff.

Perhaps it was this glare; perhaps it was the knowledge that Lad was very old and the sight of his worn-down teeth; perhaps it was the need of maintaining his hold of fear over the rebellious child. At all events, Ruloff swung aloft the belt once more and strode toward the two; balancing himself for a kick at the thundrously growling dog.

The kick did not land. For, even as Sonya cried out in new terror, Lad launched himself at the Slav.

All unprepared for the clash, and being an utter coward at heart—if he had a heart—the father reeled back, under the impact. Losing his balance, he tumbled prone to earth.

By the time his back struck ground, Lad was upon him; ravening uselessly at the swarthy throat.

But, yelling with fright, Ruloff fended him off; and twisted and writhed out of reach; bunching his feet under him and, in a second, staggering up and racing for the shelter of the nearest tree.

Up the low-stretching branches the man swarmed, until he was well out of reach. Then, pausing in his climb, he shook his fist down at the collie, who was circling the tree in a vain attempt to find some way of climbing it.

Chattering, mouthing, gibbering like a monkey, Ruloff shook an impotent fist at the dog that had treed him; and squalled insults at him and at the hysterically delighted child.

Sonya rushed up to Lad, flinging her arms around him and trying to kiss him. At her embrace, the collie's tension relaxed. He turned his back on the jabbering Ruloff, and looked pantingly up into the child's excited face.

Then, whimpering a little under his breath, he licked her cheek; and made shift to wag his plumed tail in reassurance. After which, having routed the enemy and done what he could to comfort the rescued, Laddie moved heavily over to the veranda.

For some reason he was finding it hard to breathe. And his heart was doing amazing things against his ribs. He was very tired—very drowsy. He wanted to finish his interrupted nap. But it was a long way into the house. And a spot on the veranda, under the wide hammock, promised coolness. Thither he went; walking more and more slowly.

At the hammock, he looked back: Ruloff was shinnying down from the tree; on the far side. All the fight, all the angry zest for torturing, seemed to have gone out of the man. Without so much as glancing toward Sonya or the dog, he made his way, in a wide detour, toward the barn and lunch.

Sonya ran up on the veranda after Lad. As he laid himself heavily down, under the hammock, she sat on the floor beside him; taking his head in her lap, stroking its silken fur and beginning to sing to him in that high-pitched crooning little voice of hers.

Laddie loved this. And he loved the soft caress of her hand. It soothed him to sleep.

It was good to sleep. He had just undergone more vehement exertion and excitement than had been his for many a long month. And he had earned his rest. It was sweet to doze like this—petted and sung to.

It was not well to exercise body and emotions as he had just done. Lad realized that, now;—now that it was all over and he could rest. Rest! Yes, it was good to rest,—to be smoothed and crooned at. It was thus the Mistress had stroked and crooned to him, so many thousand times. And always Lad had loved it.

It was well to be at home and to be sinking so pleasantly to sleep; here at the Place he had guarded since before he could remember—the Place where he and the Mistress and the Master had had such splendid times; where he and his long-dead mate, Lady, had romped; where he had played with and trained his fiery little son, Wolf; and where every inch of the dear land was alive with wonderful memories to him.

He had had a full, happy, rich life. And now, in its twilight, rest was as grateful as action once had been.

The morning air was warm and it was heavy with flower and field, scents; and with the breath of the forests where so often Lad had led the tearing run of the collie pack and in whose snowy depths he once had fought for his life against Wolf and the huge crossbreed, Rex. That was ever so long ago.

The Mistress and the Master were coming home. Lad knew that. He could not have told how he knew it. In earlier years, he had known their car was bringing them home to him, while it was still a mile or more distant from the Place;—had known and had cantered forth to meet it.

He was too tired, just now, to do that. At least, until he had slept for a moment or two. Always, until now, the Mistress and the Master had been first, with Lad. Now, for some odd reason, sleep was first.

And he slept;—deeply, wearily.

Presently, as he slept, he sighed and then quivered a little. After that, he lay still. The great heart, very quietly, had stopped beating.

Into the driveway, from the main road, a furlong above, rolled the homecoming car. At sight of it, Sonya started up. She was not certain how the car's occupants would take her preempting of the veranda in their absence. Letting Lad's head gently down to the floor, she slipped away.

To the barn she went, ignorant that her father had not returned to the orchard. She wanted to get herself into a more courageous frame of mind before meeting Ruloff. By experience she judged he would make her pay, and pay dear, for the fright the collie had given him.

Into the barn she ran, shutting fast its side door behind her. Then, midway across the dusky hay-strewn space, she came to a gasping stop. Ruloff had risen from a box on the corner, had set down his lunch pail, moved between her and the door and yanked off his brass-buckled belt.

The child was trapped. Here there was no earthly chance for escape. Here, too, thanks to the closed door, Laddie could not come to her aid. In palsied dread, she stood shaking and sobbing; as the man walked silently toward her.

Ruloff's flat face widened in a grin of anticipation. He had a big score to pay. And he was there to pay it. The fear of the dog was still upon him; and the shame that this child, the cause of all his humiliation, should have seen him run yelling up a tree. It would take a mighty good flogging to square that.

Sonya cried out, in mortal terror, at his first step. Then—probably only in her hysterical imagination, though afterward she vowed it had actually happened—came rescue.

Distinctly, against her quivering side, she felt the pressure of a warm furry bulk. Into her paralyzed hand a reassuring cold muzzle was thrust. And, over her, came a sense of wonderful safety from all harm. Facing her father with a high-pitched loud laugh of genuine courage, she shrilled:

"You don't dare touch me! You don't dare lay one finger on me!"

And she meant it. Her look and every inflection of the defiant high voice proved she meant it; proved it to the dumfounded Ruloff, in a way that sent funny little shivers down his spine.

The man came to a shambling halt; aghast at the transfigured little wisp of humanity who confronted him in such gay fearlessness.

"Why don't I dare?" he blustered, lifting the brass-buckled weapon again.

"You don't dare to!" she laughed, wildly. "You don't dare, because you know he'll kill you, This time he won't just knock you down. He'll *kill* you! He'll never let you hit me again. I know it. He's *here!* You don't dare touch me! You won't ever dare touch me! He—"

She choked, in her shout of weird exultation. The man, ridden by his racial superstition, stared open-mouthed at the tiny demon who screeched defiance at him.

And, there, in the dim shadows of the barn, his overwrought fancy seemed to make out a grim formless Thing, close at the child's side; crouching in silent menace.

The heat of the day—the shock of seeing Lad appear from nowhere and stand thus, by the veranda, a few minutes earlier—these and the once-timid Sonya's confident belief in Lad's presence,—all wrought on the stupid, easily-thrilled mind of the Slav.

"The werewolf!" he babbled; throwing down the belt, and bolting out into the friendly sunlight.

"The werewolf! I—I saw it! I—at least—God of Russia, what *did* I see? What did *she* see?"

Over a magnificent lifeless body on the veranda bent the two who had loved Lad best and whom he had served so worshipfully for sixteen years. The Mistress's face was wet with tears she did not try to check. In the Master's throat was a lump that made speech painful. For the tenth time he leaned down and laid his fingers above the still heart of the dog; seeking vainly for sign of fluttering.

"No use!" he said, thickly, harking back by instinct to a half-remembered phrase. "The engine has broken down."

"No," quoted the sobbing Mistress, wiser than he. "'The engineer has left it.'"

THE END